The Truth

My Journey to the Other Side

The Truth

My Journey to the Other Side

dee delaney

GARNET
PRESS

The information provided in this book is designed to provide helpful information on the subjects discussed. This book is not meant to be used, nor should it be used, to diagnose or treat any medical condition. The author and publisher are not responsible for any specific health needs that may require medical supervision and are not liable for any damages or negative consequences from any treatment, action, application, or preparation, to any person reading or following the information in this book.

References are provided for information purposes only and do not constitute endorsement of any websites or other sources. In the event you use any of the information in this book for yourself, the author, and the publisher assume no responsibility for your actions.

The Truth: My Journey to the Other Side
Dee Delaney
Tradepaper ISBN: 978-1-945026-42-3

Library of Congress Control Number: 2018939681

Published by Garnet Press

Printed in the United States of America

Table of Contents

To my stars

Millie & Fionn

PROLOGUE

Living From The Heart

When we live from the heart, we live from a place of truth and honesty; a place where we don't judge others or ourselves. This is a place of freedom, which isn't bound by rigid belief systems that tell us we can and cannot behave in a certain way. We live from a place of compassion and empathy, where we accept what is given to us and view everything with great wisdom, understanding that there is always something better to come so long as we keep the faith and trust in life. We live from a place that unifies us as equals; we see the beauty in everything around us, and we live from a place where we are open to receive our blessings as we create a life worth living. We live in the pure light of love that is within us.

This is what living from the heart means to me, and this is who I am today. I am a woman of the world and I am living in my power in the jungle in Southern India, where I am raising my little boy and writing my stories. Each day I put one foot in front of the other and accept what life brings to me with an open and loving heart. I am at peace with my life and my story.

But it wasn't always like this.

My journey has been long and hard and filled with endless loss as I spent years searching outside myself for happiness. By the age of 41, I had everything – or so I believed. I was living the Western dream that I thought everyone wanted. My life was consumed with doing. I had the job, the house, the children, the husband and the money. I was a woman driven by ambition and achievement, who struggled to get it all, and who worked damn hard to keep it. But in what I thought was a cruel twist of fate, just when I thought I had it all, the ground beneath me opened up and the life I knew and loved ended. I thought I'd lost everything, but actually it was just the beginning.

This is my story, but it is also a universal story of love and loss. It is a story that I hope will give you, the reader, the strength to believe that love is stronger than death and has the power to heal the darkest wounds and the deepest despair. Through my story I share a pathway to healing the self. It's for those who want to live in peace, and for those who want to learn how to be. It is a pathway without guilt, shame or regret. It is a path to love.

And so it begins.

PART ONE

One Woman's Story

1
Cracking Open

"In this story of one woman is the story of every woman. May you find the pathway into the spirit by which it was written." [1]

My journey back to mySelf started the day my beloved husband Tony died of a heart attack on Saturday 26th June 2010, while doing a charity walk in Scotland. Suddenly life as I knew it stopped and everything came into question.

You see, on paper I was pretty much living the dream. I met my husband in 2002 on a blind date, and I knew instantly that I had met 'the one'. Our stories were so similar. We were from Irish backgrounds, in our mid-thirties, and we both had failed relationships that had produced a child each. Tony had a son called Nicholas, who was 14 when we met, and I had my daughter Millie, who was 4. There were no buts with Tony, it was easy, and I suddenly had this love that made me feel complete. We married on 26th August 2004 in an extravagant wedding in Ireland and settled into the middle-class suburban dream in St Albans, England, a desirable commuter town just outside London. It was somewhere I had dreamed of living since I was a little girl. We both had executive jobs – he was at KPMG, I was at the BBC – and between us we pulled in a juicy six-figure salary that paid for five holidays a year and an enviable lifestyle. Life was good. Tony was a kind, gentle man, and in our short time together he showed me what it was to be loved completely. He stood by as I chased my dreams, understanding that I was ambitious and that I measured happiness by success and needed to fill every moment with doing. I was a superwoman with a tick list as long as my arm: Run the London Marathon – tick (I crawled round in 2007); have a baby – tick (our beautiful son Fionn was born on 7th August 2008); get a degree – tick (I got my Masters in Business Administration in 2009 while also working full-time at the BBC). Life was good.

Tony used to bring our son to business school in between lectures so that I could breastfeed – I was unstoppable. And when I completed everything he asked, “What next, Dee? Isn’t it time to just live?” I don’t know, perhaps he could see what was coming. We finished renovations on our dream house on 25th June 2010, it was the final tick. The next day he was dead. In the blink of an eye our life together was over before we had even really got started. I had achieved so much, but what for?

My beautiful husband was gone and I was left to pick up the pieces.

I put on the veil, shut myself down and went back to work after two short months. I was determined that grief wouldn't define me. You see, I had been there the year before. Martyn, my daughter's father, had killed himself on 21st March 2009. I had dealt with the loss then, I could deal with this now. But losing Martyn was Millie's pain, not mine. Martyn and I may have had a daughter together but we had separated long ago, he didn't live in my heart like Tony did. Losing Tony was like losing myself, and my whole existence became blurred.

I felt like this terrible dark cloud had penetrated every cell of my body, and with it came an anger that was raw and unforgiving. How could God do this to me? Tony was meant to be my happy ever after; this hadn't been part of the fucking plan! I was resentful of other people's happiness, and I had a desperate need to numb the pain, running from it through an increasing reliance on alcohol and a string of bad relationships that left me questioning my judgement and added more suffering to my life. And there was another cruel twist to come. In 2011, our little baby boy Fionn was diagnosed with cerebral palsy , just a year after Tony's death. I blamed myself entirely for his condition, because I had ruptured my placenta while gardening when I was 29 weeks pregnant, and my son's brain had been starved of oxygen. My anger now had a fresh target, and I had an almighty fight on my hands to accept my little boy's condition and to forgive myself for his health problems.

My soul was bleeding. My everyday life had become such a burden that it was difficult to see out of the fog and find the light, but somehow, through it all, I was determined to shine. And so, I started to put my life back together one tiny step at a time, and I did this by practicing yoga on a daily basis and reading every spiritual book I could get my hands on. I became a yoga teacher, gave up the BBC job in 2011 and taught yoga for three years, but something was missing. I was still trying to control life, and I felt stuck and exhausted. And there was yet still more to come. A third partner Paul, who I dated briefly for 2 years died unexpectedly in 2014. He was a secret alcoholic, and I walked out of that relationship 3 months pregnant knowing that I could not keep the baby. I made the agonizing decision to return my unborn child back to Spirit, and buried all the shame and guilt deep into the recesses of my womb. But when Paul died the embers of suffering started to feed my soul. His death was yet another nail in the coffin, if you pardon the pun, that sent me on a downward spiral of questioning and self-loathing. Suddenly I was faced with the shocking reality that I had 2 children, and a child in spirit by 3 fathers and they were all dead. All young men in their 40s, they had all died suddenly and unexpectedly in what should have been the prime of their lives. And they were all connected to me. How could this be? It seemed that death had a way of finding me and was clearly trying to teach me something about life, but at the time I just didn't understand what it could be. My soul was utterly wounded by my story, by the trinity of death that crossed my path, and I felt ashamed, damaged and somehow cursed as a new level of darkness entered my world and consumed my very being.

Then, on 21st March 2015, I stopped. I'd had enough. I was on my knees and broken as I looked to the heavens and cried, "I can't do this anymore, what am I supposed to do?" It was at this moment that I got out my pen and notebook and started to write. I had this feeling that I can only describe as an inner knowing; a voice who has always been there to guide me, but one I had ignored through my own pain and suffering. And now she was calling out to be heard. She is the wisdom within who never gives up on us. As she whispered, "Write, Dee, you must write every day," I gave my trust to her and followed her guidance. In the beginning, it was agonisingly hard to sit at my desk staring into the abyss of my soul's story, and the sadness in my heart penetrated every word on the page. Despite how difficult it was, I kept the faith and carried on writing. And in the moments of sadness I felt the divine wisdom hold my heart as she whispered, "It's OK, Dee, it's going to be OK." This beautiful voice of the Divine that started to flow through my words had a plan for me. She was calling me to write my story for a higher purpose that was beyond my understanding at the time. She was calling me to be healed, and as I cried a thousand tears onto the pages, I opened my heart and finally let go of all the pain and suffering I had carried for years. I could feel the healing light of love in my heart and, as I awakened to its presence, it became increasingly clear that I had been guided by a divine truth all my life; a truth that showed itself the night before Tony died and was there to protect and prepare me for the road ahead. This truth is connected to the inner light inside us all, if only we had eyes that could see and ears that could hear it. There is only one truth but there are many paths to it, and here in my story, I share with you mine.

2

Growing Up

"It takes courage to grow up and become who you really are."

E.E. Cummings

I was born into a world of love and confusion. It was a world of conformity, Catholicism and pleasing others, where being seen to do the right thing was everything. My father was lost to drink and my mother raised four children without complaining, doing her best out of duty and necessity, as she buried her dreams and made the most of her lot. My birth name was Dolores Ann Fallon. It was a name that made me cringe, and a name that I always denied. I never really understood why, until years later, when I realised how disconnected I was from this world that I had chosen to enter.

"Your father should never have married," was Mum's opening line whenever we discussed the past and his downfalls. She was just 17 when she fell pregnant with my twin brothers,

Adrian and Patrick, and both she and my Dad were sent to England to get married, as having children out of wedlock in 1960s Ireland was not the done thing. A year later, my sister Susan was born and I arrived a year after that – on 30th May 1969. This all happened before Mum hit 20 and she raised the four of us pretty much singlehandedly.

My dad, Patsy Fallon, was, by his own admission, a lovable rogue. He was happiest when he was propping up a bar telling his famous stories to any passing waif or stray. Charismatic, intelligent and generous, everybody loved Patsy. In the 70s and 80s he ran his own successful building company and employed lots of local men. He was a central figure in the Irish community in our hometown of Watford in the UK, and was heavily involved in Gaelic hurling and football. I was raised with strong, working-class Irish values, to work hard, show good manners and obey our mother. We were punished if we failed to do as we were told. This didn't involve anything too brutal, there was the odd slap or strike with the back of a slipper, but it definitely reminded me of my place in life. As the youngest in the family, I also knew I was the last in the pecking order.

Life in our household was very routine. During the week, Mum would cook the exact same food. Monday was stew, Tuesday was bacon and cabbage, Wednesday was chicken, Thursday was a fry up and Friday was fish and chips. Saturday was, as she put it, her 'day off' so she didn't cook a hot meal.

Instead she would bake the most delicious cakes, scones and 'mammie's soda bread' and we would have filled rolls from the bakery. Sunday was a big roast dinner. Week in, week out, it was always the same. Meals were served at 6pm, except on Sunday when the roast was dished up at 3pm. You could set your watch by it. And boy did I love my mum's dinners. She was a fantastic cook and we always ate every morsel on our plates. There was no other food or snacks in the house so we either ate what was given to us or went hungry. Dad worked six days a week and went to the pub every day without fail. Mum would leave his dinner sitting on the side and he'd eat it when he came home, by which time we'd all be in bed. On Saturday night we all went to the Irish club. Dad would prop up the bar and Mum would dance the night away with her friends. I cherished those Saturday evenings. I loved to spin around the dance floor doing the waltz or twist and turn like a lightning bolt while taking part in a jive. On Sundays, we slightly begrudgingly went to mass. We were not a particularly religious family and I was never encouraged to pray at bedtime or read the Bible, but we had to be 'seen' at church.

"Make sure the priest sees you," Mum would say.

Attending mass was her way of showing the world she was doing a good job and raising her children in the Catholic faith, which was important to her. Dad was less bothered. He'd go if he felt like it, or if Mum made him, but he didn't care so much about being seen to be doing the right thing. Sunday afternoon was the highlight of my week as we visited our extended family for tea and cake in Luton, the town next to ours. It was a rare moment of family unity and was a chance for me to be a child again as I played with my cousins and watched my mum looking happy for a few short hours as she caught up with her four sisters. This was also a way of getting Dad away from the pub and being a real father. He had to take us to Luton in his green work van – which we aptly named 'The Green Goddess' – because mum couldn't drive and catching the bus with four children was not her idea of a fun afternoon out. But she had to beg him every week to take us. His reluctance wasn't because he didn't enjoy spending time with his family, but because he didn't like being too far away from the pub. We would arrive around 4pm and an hour and a half later he would be getting restless and trying to gather us all up to leave. Then he would drive at lightning speed down the motorway in time for opening hours. On Monday, Dad would head to work at 6am then go straight to the pub until closing time, losing himself in drink once again. And that was our family life. My dad wasn't unkind, aggressive or difficult, he was simply lost to his love of booze. And I felt that loss deeply in my heart and wanted him to be different. I wanted my dad to be 'normal' and, as I grew older and compared my life to the lives of my friends, I developed a very clear sense of what I thought 'normal' should be. I wanted a dad who came home from work early, gave me cuddles without the accompanying smell of stale beer, read me a story at bedtime, tucked me up, told me he loved me, took an interest in my education and wanted to teach me to ride a bike. This person didn't have to be extraordinary in any way. He just had to want to do 'dad' things.

> *"A mother is truly Divine. It is from her womb that we have emerged…this means treating her with respect, with love, with patience."* [2]

Mum rarely showed how desperately sad she was, despite spending many a night crying herself to sleep and looking out of the window wondering where her husband was. She was a silent martyr and cared and loved us with everything she had. We were her world and her pride and joy, and somehow I turned into a silent martyr just like her. I could see she was struggling so I wanted to ease her burden. I became the good girl who helped in the house and cleaned up after everyone when she was too exhausted to do it. I also dragged the weekly shopping home from town because Dad was never around to help her. I stepped in where he should have been. And I did the same for him. I helped him with his business accounts and paperwork when it got out of control, which it often did. It was as if I'd been propelled into the family to be of service. I never complained, but I watched on in silent judgement, as my inner voice questioned everything around me. I hid my true feelings behind an innocent smile that just accepted that this was how life was. I was never encouraged to speak my mind or be ambitious. Life was about getting through the drudgery of day-to-day existence. Money – namely the lack of it – was always an issue. Once we were at school, Mum took a job as a dinner lady so she'd have a bit of pocket money – Dad was never that reliable with the finances. I attended a good Roman Catholic school run by a few nuns. They were heavy handed on the discipline front and would punish us if our skirts weren't below the knee or if our hair wasn't neatly kept. I was terrified of the church and the Catholic doctrine that had been fed to me since birth. I always winced when I looked up at Jesus on the cross and questioned the loving nature of God, especially when one of the nuns pulled my hair to silence me if she felt I was being too proud or loud. How could they be considered honourable when they behaved in such a way? There was so much judgement and double standards in the church, but I dutifully attended mass and swallowed the words of the Bible without ever fully believing in them.

Despite taking on a part-time job, Mum never had any spare cash to buy us little extras. We were not poor by any standard, but when I went to school and saw where all the other kids lived and how they had bikes and music lessons and nice holidays and went to restaurants with their parents, I started to see a life that I wanted. I wanted the middle-class life like all my friends, not the working-class one I had. I felt embarrassed by our little two-up two-down terrace, which was tiny compared with my contemporaries' beautiful suburban semis. And I judged myself as not being worthy of their friendship. I kept to myself and was never invited over for sleepovers, I began to isolate myself and nurture my growing lack of self-worth. This sense of not feeling good enough shaped my whole teenage years and had a huge impact on my relationships with others, particularly men. I remember once pleading with my mum to pay for ballet lessons, but she couldn't afford them. She could see how upset I was as I watched my friends skip off in their beautiful pink tutus and I know this weighed heavily on her – no parent wants to see their child miss out. She wanted to give us the best, but what could she do? She grew up at a time when women lacked financial freedom. They married young, often out of necessity, and were expected to stay at home with the children while the 'man of the house' basically went about his business as he pleased. Mum's own mother lived that way, as did her grandmother and no doubt countless other women down her family line. This was just how it was. But the path Mum was on wasn't the one she wanted for her daughters.

"You must always have your own money," she'd remind us whenever she could. "Don't ever rely on a man."

It was too late for her to live by that mantra, but her advice certainly helped to shape me into the woman I am today. I have a generation of Jackson women to thank for my fierce independence and my desire to be self-sufficient come what may. And so the struggles in my teenage years planted the seed for the life I wanted: the middle-class life that my school friends had, with the nice house, the 2.4 kids and the professional husband. I was determined to be the one to break the mould and close the door on the emotional turmoil of the life I'd been born into.

Meanwhile, Mum didn't feel she had the strength to make a change and remained in her marriage for 20 years. Throughout this whole period, she was nursing a broken heart. When us kids were little she had met a man at the Irish club and had fallen desperately in love. This man was also married with a young family, and although they pined to be together, neither could face the prospect of breaking up their respective lives. So, they agreed to 'do the right thing' by sacrificing their own happiness and staying away from each other. Their paths crossed frequently – the Irish community in Watford was a tight circle of people – and it must have been so difficult for them to resign themselves to separate married lives while being so desperately in love. But they couldn't live out the pretence forever – love always finds a way to surface – and by the time I was 18, Mum's marriage to Dad had started to implode. She'd had enough. Dad's drinking had become increasingly out of control, and in the last few years of their time together he just seemed to give up. Bills remained unpaid, the house was close to being repossessed and his building business went bankrupt. Mum didn't want to know. She'd pretty much given up too. She made her mind up that she'd paid her dues and now it was time for her to find some happiness.

She saw my coming of age, her youngest child, as her gateway to freedom. Throughout the darkest days of her marriage, she had promised herself she would stick with my dad through it all, but only until her children were all old enough to stand on their own two feet. And for her that time came when I reached adulthood. And, although I was still at college and needed my mum, the inner strength she saw in me gave her the confidence to start a new life.

While my brothers and sister were working and had lives outside of the house and long-term partners to turn to, I was on my own. Mum had threatened to go many times, and even packed her bags and left, only to return 30 minutes later after missing her bus. This time, though, there was no turning back. She was terrified of what her family and the church would say and didn't know how she would cope being on her own. She used to come up to my bed late at night, cry on my shoulder and seek my advice. I never once thought about the impact this was having on me, I simply sat, listened and provided comfort. Mum was like a little child. I could see that her fear ran deep, but I also empathised with her need to find happiness. She used to say I was more like a mother to her than she was to me.

With just the clothes on her back, she was scared and lonely, but she finally had her freedom. This came at a price, though, and in those early days after she left, Mum had many dark moments as she battled with guilt, carrying the shame of a generation of women who did the unthinkable and left their husbands and families. Inevitably, the struggle took its toll on her health, but she eventually grew stronger and never gave up on romance. She was finally free to be with the man she had fallen in love with all those years earlier . They are now happily settled together in Ireland. They live in a house two doors down from where Mum grew up and have just celebrated their 27th anniversary. I truly believe Mum has come full circle and is finally where she should be.

Dad was furious when Mum left. He never actually believed she would do it, despite her years spent threatening to, and he just wasn't ready to accept responsibility for himself, so he directed his anger at me. He blamed me for helping her leave and in a fit of rage kicked me out of the house, telling me he never wanted to see me again. He seemed to have forgotten the nights I'd held him as he cried on my shoulder in drunken despair, knowing the marriage was over. Instead of gratitude for my help, there I was at 19, in the middle of my college exams, with an absent mum and a dad who had made me homeless. I was on my own and had been abandoned by the two people in the world who I should have been able to rely on. It felt as if everything was falling apart around me. My siblings, who had never known about Mum's intention to leave, were deeply shocked, and they dealt with their pain in their own separate ways. Adrian and Susan had moved out to live with their partners and get on with their lives while Patrick stayed with Dad and tried to steady the ship before the inevitable happened and the house was repossessed. Without Mum to pull us all together, our family just sort of disintegrated. I saw very little of my brothers and sister in those early days after she left. Dad hit the bottle hard and refused to speak to me, despite my efforts to hold out an olive branch and make some peace. Mum also went off the radar for a while. She needed time alone to grieve for her marriage and family, and to pick over the pieces of her life as she tried to make sense of what had gone wrong. And so, for the first time in my life, I was on my own.

With very little money, I moved to London to start a new life. For a while I moved about a lot. The worst place I stayed was a squat in Brixton, South London. It was freezing cold, had no running water and the boys I shared with organised impromptu raves and trashed the place – not that there was much to trash. It was a pretty grim time. I eventually moved to a comfortable flat in Islington, got a job at an advertising agency and worked hard to provide for myself. But as someone who learnt how to love through helping others, I became desperate to please and struggled with setting boundaries I found it hard to stand my ground at work and say no, so I ended up doing more than my fair share of long hours and early mornings, which eventually took a physical toll on me. I became resentful of work and hated living in London. I had never felt so lonely or lost in my entire life. When my work colleagues left in the evening to be with their families, it only reminded me how I didn't have anywhere to call home. At the time, I didn't know how to express my feelings or talk about my past. I kept my parents' ugly separation a secret and covered up just how much I was hurting inside. Without that strong foundation of family love and support, I struggled to know how to say enough was enough. Instead I lived behind the façade of my carefully constructed persona – and she needed to be perfect. During a two-year stint of excessive exercise and bulimic purging, I forced my body into being a perfect size 8. I was in a constant state of anger, sadness and frustration, and I turned these emotions on myself as I abused my body. It was a horrendous time. I felt I was going insane and was ashamed about what I was doing to myself, which only fed into my cycle of self-loathing. There was no space to breathe. I strictly controlled calorie intake before trying to burn them off with hours of running, swimming and cycling followed by another purge to make sure nothing stayed in my system. Being bulimic is a truly horrifying way to live and by the time I was 21, the tortuous hours of exercise and constant control of my diet had taken their toll and I was almost at breaking point. I gave up my job at the ad agency and went to stay with Mum, who at this time was living close to her sisters in Luton. I trained to become a croupier at the local casino and saved every penny to go travelling, which I saw as my big 'way out'.

Meanwhile, I continued to be consumed with hatred. I hated living in Luton and was desperately unhappy. I carried on with my gruelling training sessions for another six months before coming home one day and breaking down.

"I can't do this anymore," I screamed at mum.

She couldn't hide her shock. She had never seen me vulnerable, and suddenly here I was broken for the first time. I'd given up the façade and self-control and for the first time in years I let the anger surface and asked for help. In the summer of 1990, I went to see a therapist. As I opened up, her response spoke directly to my soul.

"Dee you're an adult now and you make mistakes and that's OK," she said. "Your parents are also adults and they make mistakes too."

Her words really resonated with me. I knew I was being called to show compassion and forgiveness to my parents for my childhood experiences. And to some extent I did. But I failed to see this message was actually a call for me to make peace with myself. It was an opportunity for me to grow up, release my resentment and anger and move on. Unfortunately, I was still stuck in a pattern of looking outwards. I lived behind the veil of the good girl and fixated on helping others, dishing out advice and judging people. It was only when I had therapy again years later that I learnt how my behaviour was a coping mechanism to try and control life, and I'd actually been in deep denial about my childhood and still held onto many painful feelings that needed to be released.

After seeing the therapist, I decided I wanted to try to make amends with my dad. I was about to go travelling and decided to see him before I left. We met in a local pub and he looked a bit sheepish. I think he was probably hungover from the night before. Rather naively, the first thing he said to me was, "You've put on a bit of weight, Dolores."

OMG! The man hadn't seen me for two years and the first thing he did was call me fat. I was utterly floored. I mean, really, surely all men know they're walking into dangerous territory if they comment on a woman's weight, let alone a woman who is recovering from bulimia? But Dad wasn't aware of the pain that sat behind my excess pounds – he didn't know about my bulimia and my struggles. He hadn't been around to help me through that tough time in my life and his words lit the fuse that triggered the bomb inside me that had been waiting to explode. Boy did I let him have it. In an explosive rage of pure hatred and judgement, I spewed out a list of crimes as I told him what a useless father he was, and how he had constantly let me down, disappointed me, embarrassed me, and so on. He listened gobsmacked as I hurled abuse after abuse until the fire inside me had burnt out.

As a finishing remark, I looked him in the eye and said, "You haven't been the best of dads, but despite it all I love you and I forgive you."

How very big of me after I had pulled the man to pieces. That was my idea of empathy at the time. Castrate the man then say, "It's OK, I forgive you."

To his credit, Dad didn't walk away and when I had finished talking he looked at me rather solemnly and replied, "You always were the strong one. I wish your mother had stood up to me like you did."

But I was hiding behind my strength. Being strong was my coping mechanism. I put all the hurt and sadness from my childhood into a box, locked it away and got on with life. In many ways I was no different from Dad. He hid behind alcohol to ease the pain, while I hid behind strength. But, as I was to discover 25 years later when I had therapy again, whatever we lock away has to eventually find its way out.

So, at the age of 21, I closed the door on my past and backpacked around India, South East Asia and Australia to escape my misery, essentially staying on the road until I was 25. It was then that my love affair with India began. I only came back to the UK once during that period because I'd run out of money. Once home, I took on three jobs and worked every hour God sent, putting my life on hold til I'd saved up enough so to be able to return to India six months later. It was where I needed to be.

3 Moving On

"Our bodies and our brains may be in the West, but our spirit must stay with our motherland, in India." [3]

I first stepped on Indian soil after arriving in New Delhi at 4am on a British Airways flight. I was with my friend Donna and we were absolutely bloody terrified. Landing anywhere new at 4am is never a smart move, especially when you are two young British girls and look squeaky clean and very green. We were both 21 and had never been outside Europe before. It didn't help that back in the 1990s, everyone in India seemed to be out to scam you. Whenever you arrived somewhere new, you'd hear news of a curfew or, "No, Madame, there is no electricity," or, "No, Madame, there is holiday nothing is open," or, "No, Madame, there is fighting between Hindus and Muslims, it's not safe. You have to come with me and I take you to the best hotel!"

Each city had its own unique way of trying to fleece the unsuspecting tourist. Over time we became savvier to these tricks. We grew in confidence and looked noticeably dirtier – as you do when you backpack around India. On the plus side, the dirtier we got the more the scammers left us alone.

When we arrived in Delhi on that first morning we were told there was a curfew and the city was on lockdown, which meant we couldn't go to our youth hostel. The taxi drivers wanted to take us to a fancy hotel that would have blown our monthly budget in one fell swoop and left them rich in the pocket after receiving a backhander from the hotel owner. All they could see was two rich, Western tourists who between them had more money than they could possibly earn in a lifetime – and they wanted a piece of it.

I gathered some inner strength, took Donna's hand and hustled our way through the crowds and onto a local bus, which took us to the area where the youth hostel was. Needless to say, it was in the middle of nowhere. The bus driver dropped us off in the darkness of the night and said something in Hindi, which I can only assume was along the lines of, "Do you really want to stay here in the arse end of nowhere?"

I'm sure Donna was thinking the same thing, but in my mind we were intrepid explorers and I was damned if a little hiccup like a curfew was going to scupper my plans for adventure. And that's how we made our way around magical India – with a large dose of faith that all would be well and a carefree attitude that brought us the most vivid, amazing and spellbinding experiences I can still practically touch today. I fell in love – India was my country. I belonged to her and she belonged to me. I knew deeply that part of me had walked with her in a previous life and I felt guided by an Indian spirit. I had this longing for a woman who lived in colonial India, at the time of British rule. I felt her energy with me, as if she was me in another life.

I was 22 when I went back to India for the second time. This time I was on my own, just me and my backpack, and I loved the freedom of it all. Suddenly I had nobody else to please but myself. But of course, I was never really on my own for long. Backpackers follow a well-trodden route around India, searching out the hashish and party scene, as well as the temples and culture. And so, I ended up travelling in a convoy of 20 people, all from different nationalities. We were all doing our own thing but ended up following each other along the path. We spent most of our time in the temples and on the beaches of Southern India, and for the first time in my life, I felt truly happy. I was comfortable in my skin, had locked away the pain of my childhood and was finally enjoying living my freedom and caring only for myself. And, of course, I was stoned most of the time! I used to wake up to a chillum and smoke my way through the day as I glided around India on a haze of hashish, experiencing life in technicolour, and doing some crazy ass shit. I gave away all my possessions in Madura as an act of blissful detachment from materialism. I still vividly remember standing at the temple complex giving my precious Sony Walkman to the street kids and declaring I no longer needed it because I was free – I must have been really stoned that day! I camped out under the stars on Om beach in Gokarna and lived for three weeks in a hut that I'd constructed out of bamboo. I drank chai, smoked hash and swam with the dolphins at sunset. Back then, the beaches in the south were little bits of uncommercialised paradises and it was just me and my group of friends and the chai man. We travelled with our own stove and chapatti pan and would pitch up on a beach, make a fire, cook food, watch the sunset and laze around for days. I hung out at the legendary Shore Bar in Anjuna, north Goa, for months and haggled with the Rajasthani women at the Wednesday flea market, becoming part of the hippie scene and buying my drugs from a guy called Neptune who looked like he was still on a trip from the 60s. I was always level-headed enough to dip in, experiment and have my fun while knowing when it was time to take myself away. I saw too many casualties of that scene to want to do that to myself. I witnessed many Israelis party hard just to anesthetise the memory of military service only to lose themselves to heroin and acid and add more suffering.

In the village of Mahabalipurumm in Tamil Nadu, I lived in a hut made out of cow dung and had to take a stick with me to keep the pigs at bay when I went to the toilet in the field outside. I also climbed the giant boulders and explored the forlorn ruins of Hampi, which I can only describe as out of this world – to the point where I believe the gods must have had some involvement in its creation. I watched phosphorus dance in the moonlight whilst gliding down the Keralan backwaters on a houseboat, and I walked through the monsoon-soaked streets of Calcutta with water up to my knees, trying not to think of what was lurking in the soup around my ankles. India left its imprint on my heart and when it was time to leave I cried like a baby. I remember sitting on the airport floor in Calcutta and sobbing as I waited for a flight to Hong Kong, wondering when I'd be back. Little did I know it would take 25 years for me to step on Indian soil again, but when I did the country held out her arms and embraced my heart once again. It was worth the wait.

"In the sweetness of friendship let there be laughter, and sharing of pleasures. For in the dew of little things the heart finds its morning and is refreshed."

Khalil Gibran

Between the ages of 23 and 25, I lived in Hong Kong and Australia and worked as a waitress in various bars and restaurants to feed my traveling lifestyle. While in Hong Kong, I met my lifelong best friend Debbie. She was the first woman I had ever grown close to and loved. Her energy, zest for life and passion to party is the stuff of legend. She's been with me every step of the way since we met, guiding me through the rough and the smooth. She was a bridesmaid at my wedding, was the first to visit me when the kids were born and she held my hand when Tony died, wiping away my tears and looking after me through the dark times. She never questioned or judged when my behavior spiraled out of control, but was always there in the background to pick me up when I was ready to fall. She was the best friend I'd always wanted when I was a little girl. Back then I was the child on the outside looking in. I had never really connected with anyone on a deep level, had a best friend to do girly things with or go for sleepovers. But when I met Debbie all that changed and I couldn't have asked for a better friend. I truly believe the universe gives you everything you need in its own divine time. We've celebrated three milestone birthdays (our 30th, 40th and her 50th) together, and I know we'll be doing the same for the rest of our days. I'm truly grateful for the gift of her friendship. There are very few people in life that are with you every step of the way, and when we find them it's a real blessing. People come in and out of our lives for all sorts of reasons, but there is something special about a male or female friendship that endures over time. There is safety in it. For me, there is space to be me. It's a chance to come off the stage, let go of the jazz hands and be authentic.

I will also always be truly grateful for having the means and the desire to want to travel, especially when half the world lives hand to mouth and will never enjoy the same opportunities. I am reminded of that every time I am in Asia, where most people live day to day, and some never get to leave their local area, let alone step outside their country to experience life elsewhere. So I count my blessings every time I go off on an adventure. Travel feeds my soul. I always come back from a trip a better, more conscious and a more humble human being.

4
Then There Were Three

"Only I can change my life. No one can do it for me."

Carol Burnett

My first child Millie was born on 5th March 1998, and it was love at first sight. She was the child I had wanted and longed for since I was little, when all I had ever dreamt about was getting married and having children. I used to dream about her as a way of escaping the turmoil that was going on inside me as I grew up. In my dreams I was 25 and living in middle-class suburbia in a beautiful house with a dutiful husband who provided for my two children and me. It was the antithesis to the life I had growing up. I craved a stable home environment and all I ever wanted in life was to get married and start a family. When I hit 25 I came back from my travels and set about fulfilling my dream. I wanted to find a husband to settle down with and get married. Well of sorts. That was the master plan, the place I was always heading towards, but I wasn't yet done with the party scene and having fun. I worked hard in the ad agency by day and sipped vast quantities of chardonnay by night with my work friends – it was the 1990s after all. At the weekend I would hit it hard with the friends I'd met travelling. We were all back in London, living in denial and still not quite ready to leave the party. We used to head out to the Chunnel Club on Saturday nights, high on life and ecstasy, and see it through to Sunday, welcoming in the dawn of a new day by dancing away to hardcore trance music at Strawberry Sundays with a legion of other like-minded travellers. We were reminiscing about the full moon parties of Koh Phangan and trying to recreate the magic in a sweaty club under the arches of Vauxhall Bridge in South London. And this is how my life rolled. I had a foot in two camps and felt equally comfortable in both. Part of me was drawn to the bright lights of London and the heady experience of metropolitan living, which included a big job, money, a beautiful house, a fancy car, beautiful clothes and the *Sex and the City* lifestyle that saw me as a girl about town in the best bars and restaurants. But another part of me wanted to be barefoot and dirty in the sand with all the travellers and alternative people who lived at the other extreme. They were the people who lived outside the system – a creative, artsy alternative crew who wouldn't be seen dead inside an office pen pushing to feed the corporate machine. They lived for the festival scene, worked for charities or made their money through their art, or by doing a meaningful job that balanced their karma and contributed towards making the world a better place to be. Martyn, Millie's dad, was one of those people. I met him at a house party in Maida Vale that had been thrown by some friends from Hong Kong, and the attraction was instant. We got together in a haze of drink and drugs in the summer of 1996, partied the weekends away until the twilight hours and limped through the working week in eager anticipation to repeat it all again the following Friday and Saturday. That was our life together until I got pregnant and had to grow up. Martyn, on the other hand, was the boy who never grew up. He bounced around with an exuberant laugh and a zest for life that was extreme. He did everything to the max. He ate too much, drank too much and smoked too much, but he also laughed for England and was as playful as a puppy and great fun to be around. Well, he was when he was on a high. He also had the tendency to swing the other way and his life was plagued by bouts of deep depression that kept him trapped in a dark place. He worked for a charity to help rehouse homeless people and was very passionate about fixing the social injustice in the UK. He saw how the rich were getting richer while the less fortunate in society were downtrodden. He was a complete socialist lefty who believed in taxing the rich to feed the poor, and he hated the inequality of the world, which at the time favoured white, middle-class men. He was a freedom fighter for the rights of the underprivileged. He stood up for women's rights, gay rights and the rights of the homeless. His heart was in the right place but his mind was very complex. And he struggled with his demons. His friends were all similar. They were struggling artists and musicians, or they were unemployed, but they were all cut from the same cloth and wanted to live outside the system. And in some ways that was the appeal of our union. Martyn was a great antidote to the corporate life that was filling my pockets and broadening my waistband but failing to feed my soul. It was a whirlwind romance: we met, fell in love and moved in with each other within three months. I think this was more out of necessity than anything else, he had nowhere to live and was sofa surfing. But I knew ,from the moment I found out I was pregnant that my relationship wasn't going to last because it was held together by a haze of drink and drugs. The highs were very high but the lows were very low, and in the cold light of day, when I stepped out of that lifestyle due to my condition, I saw clearly that we weren't well matched. Five months into my pregnancy, I remember sobbing into Debbie's arm, as I knew I would be bringing up my daughter on my own. This was not part of the dream, the little girl's vision of happiness. I was unmarried, 20 weeks pregnant and living in a small, rented shared flat in North West London with a man I didn't love. This was actually my worst nightmare, and it was also Martyn's. I think we both knew that the relationship was never going to work, but we held on until Millie was born and stayed together for nine months afterwards as we battled with ourselves and the reality of our situation. And that reality was not pretty. Martyn was unemployed and looked after Millie full-time while I went back to work at the ad agency to provide for us. This was not how it was supposed to be. I was meant to be married and living in a nice house with my husband supporting me. Ours was not a balanced relationship, and our union was all over and done with by January 1999. Martyn went back to his hometown of Norwich, and I went to live in Luton to be close to my family. After the initial unpleasantness that comes with a separation and two years of fighting in court, which bled us dry both financially and emotionally, we eventually found our peace and became friends.

Millie is very much her father's daughter. She absolutely adored her larger-than-life dad. Her stays with him at weekends and for extended periods in the holidays were always filled with tales of great mischief. He made a big impression on her life, and although his mental health was not always stable he firmly believed that he was put on this earth to help others. He was passionate about helping the homeless and ironically his motto was, "All you need is love." Unfortunately, he never quite lived that truth for himself.

"It is not death that man should fear, he
should fear never beginning to live."

Marcus Aurelius

Martyn's life came to a tragic end on 21st March 2009. He had suffered from Bipolar disorder and ended his life by taking a massive overdose of his prescribed medication, enough to knock out a horse three times over. He looked like he meant it. The police called me late Saturday evening on 22nd March to confirm his death, and although they had to wait for the coroner's report they alluded to the fact that he had taken his own life. My beautiful little Millie was upstairs happily asleep in bed, and the next morning I knew I'd have to break the devastating news to a sweet, gentle 11-year-old girl that her beloved daddy had died. How does a person do that? I remember spending the night shaking with fear. I was so scared of the hurt and pain I was about to bring to her, and fearful of what words to choose. I didn't know how to say it was suicide. How would I explain to a little child that an adult could be so desperate and so unhappy that they might want to take their own life? How could I bring reason, logic and compassion to something that I could barely comprehend myself? And worse of all, I knew what I had to do would break her spirit.

The next day was Mothering Sunday and, bless her, Millie hopped into my bedroom all excited to give me my present and make me breakfast in bed. Instead I had to sit her down and tell her the worst news imaginable. I will never ever forget that moment. The shock on her face, the moment of denial, the moment of questioning – "No, it can't be true, Mummy, it can't be possible" – and then the soul-shattering moment of reality when she realised it was true and let out a heart-bursting, guttural scream that pierced my very being. I've only ever heard that scream one other time before, and it came from my soul the day my Tony died.

"Be Western (if you live in the West) when it comes to professional excellence but be Indian in your domestic life and in your heart."[4]

I joined the BBC at the same time as my relationship with Martyn ended, remaining there for 14 years. I had to find a way of juggling work, commuting and being a single mum. Before joining the BBC I was working round the clock in advertising agencies but there was no way I could sustain a media lifestyle with a newborn child. I couldn't just get up and leave the office every day at 5pm while my team worked late into the night (which was common practice at ad agencies back in the 90s). And I wasn't prepared to compromise spending time at home with my daughter in the evenings. She was just too precious for that. Advertising wasn't your average nine to five kind of job and I was the first working mum at the agency and at the time I had to break down barriers to get a four-day week contract. Everyone said the agency would never give the contract to me, but they did. And I'm proud to have played a part in setting the way for other working mums at the agency. But I hated walking out of the door at 5pm, and I hated missing out on all the social events that went hand-in-hand with my job, such as popping over the road to the local pub for a post-work drink and a chinwag, or going out on numerous corporate events, or jollies as we used to call them. This was very much part of the ad scene back in the 1990s. So when I stumbled across the ad for the job at the BBC in the *Media Guardian*, I put an application in at the last minute and thought nothing of it. And much to my surprise, I got the job. I was the perfect candidate for the role, but dare I say, I think I might have been the only candidate who applied! But I came at a price. I wasn't prepared to move without getting what I wanted. So I asked for a 25% pay increase, a four-day working week, and an understanding that I would leave work at 5pm every day. I insisted they gave me access to the network so I could work from home one day a week, and I basically wanted to keep my own schedule. It was a pretty ballsy. I wasn't attached to the outcome, I had a perfectly good job, so I had nothing to lose. I figured I could stand my ground and ask for what I wanted. And they acquiesced to all my demands. Working at the BBC was a huge blessing when it came to the minefield that was being a working mum in the 1990s. I'm sure a lot of women will understand when I say I constantly felt compromised for wanting to have a meaningful career whilst wishing to spend quality time at home raising my daughter. I grew up with feminism as my standard, and a culture that was almost insistent that women should go out to work and prove themselves. My peers and I couldn't be content with staying at home, having babies and being supported by our husbands. That would have been a real crime back in my day. We had to pave the way for a generation of women and show the world we could have it all. It was a badge of honour to the sisterhood to be absolutely on your knees and ravaged with exhaustion as you held down a full-time power job, raised 2.4 perfect kids, cooked a Michelin-starred meal for the hubby, arranged a full social life for the kids after school, with activities such as mandarin and violin lessons, and planned culturally enriching weekends for the grownups, including trips to the theatre and wine tasting. I'm bloody exhausted just thinking about it. But this is how I lived my life back then. I was on the conveyer belt of doing and achieving so much on the outside, but I had little conscious awareness of what was happening on the inside. I was driven by ambition, and if I'm honest I measured my happiness in money, achievement and fitting in with the social norm. And anyway, I had very little choice in the early days. I was a single mum with a child to raise and a mortgage to pay.

And although I loved my work, those early years of Millie's life were very difficult. I hated living in Luton and I hated being on my own. It was a very dark time. I never wanted to be a single mum, and here I was at 30 living in a town I had fled nearly a decade earlier. I felt like I was back at the beginning, and I was deeply wounded. How could this be? This wasn't part of the plan. My Catholic upbringing had left me feeling very ashamed of my single-mum status, and my lack of self-worth and the issues from my childhood still lurked deep inside my soul and were calling to be healed. I wanted nothing more than to meet a nice man to take me away from it all, and to support my daughter and me. But we don't attract nice men when we are in the depths of darkness – we attract the not-so-nice men, and believe it or not it was my father who introduced me to the next one, and that relationship turned out to be an absolute disaster. I should have known really. He was a secret alcoholic just like my dad. Another wounded soul I tried to fix. Everyone around me at the time knew the relationship was all wrong, as did I, but somehow being with him seemed better than being on my own. It wasn't. He hid behind his alcohol addiction, which he managed to keep it a secret for 18 months, or maybe I just didn't want to see it. Then, one day, I got into the car with him, his two daughters and Millie, and he was so drunk that he could barely keep the car on the road. I managed to pull the steering wheel out of his hands and swerve the car onto a grass verge, as we were about to approach a busy motorway. It was a very dark time for me and I was also 3 months pregnant with his child, but the near accident gave me the strength to leave and we parted company that day and I never saw him again. Paul never recovered from his addictions and he died in 2014 from an alcohol-related illness. He was in his mid-40s.

I decided not to keep the baby, and I locked away the shame and guilt of that time in the deepest, darkest recesses of my soul. I focused on taking care of myself and Millie and for the first time in years I stopped looking outside for happiness and was content to be on my own. I actually remember the heaviness shifting from my heart when I closed my door at night and thanked God the relationship with Paul was over. I felt this overwhelming sense of peace and love because I'd had the courage to walk away. And for the first time in years I was actually happy – genuinely hand-on-heart happy. And this happiness was met in the most poetic of ways. It was only when I stopped searching for love outside of myself, and started feeding the love within me, that the door opened and a new man walked in. It turned out that the universe hadn't given up on me. Just two months after Paul walked out of my life, Tony, my beloved husband, walked in.

"Someone I once loved gave me a box full of darkness.
It took me years to understand that this, too, was a gift"

Mary Oliver

I met Tony Delaney on Saturday 14th September 2002 at The Pines Hotel in Luton. We were introduced by mutual friends who were keen to do some matchmaking, and had an inkling that we would be perfect together. I was so relieved to have been released from my relationship with Paul and happy to be living on my own again with my little girl, that the last thing I cared about was letting someone else into my life. Of course, all that changed when Tony Delaney walked into the bar. I can honestly say that it was love at first sight. Tony was wearing cream cords, a brown linen shirt and his hair was speckled grey. He was 6ft2, handsome, Irish and nervous. He walked with his head down and his right fist clenched. I could feel his energy straight away. If I close my eyes and go into my heart I can still summon him up. It's as if he walked through that door only yesterday. That is the ultimate blessing of the love we shared.

We had some drinks and went on to a Chinese restaurant, where I spent the evening poking him with chopsticks, which he complained was mildly annoying, but that didn't stop him sneaking a kiss in the back of the taxi on the way home. He came back to my house and we stayed up all night talking and sharing stories about our pasts. It seemed like we had travelled a similar path and by the morning I pretty much knew that I wanted to spend the rest of my life with this man. Tony knew it instantly too, and although he was unattached, he did have a loose thing going on with a girl whom I called 'the Kiwi'. She was from New Zealand, and I never did find out her real name. He was meeting her later that day to see The Lion King on stage in London – it was his favourite show and he'd seen it four times already. I made a point of telling him that he could only have my number if he dumped 'the Kiwi'. We laughed about it, but I remember him looking me in the eye and saying, very sincerely, "Dee, I'm not one for playing games, so yes, I would love your number." And boy did I make sure he had it. I gave him a small piece of paper containing my home number, my work number, my mobile number and my email address – he took the paper and laughed when he saw the list of contacts. There was no way I was letting him get away.

"I guess I have no excuses then," he said.

After that day we were pretty much inseparable. He dumped 'the Kiwi', came round every night for three weeks straight and had moved in by January 2003. We were engaged by May and we married the following year, on 26th August 2004. Tony was my husband, my friend, my soul mate, my everything.

We danced the dance of married life with mutual respect for each other and flowed with the ups and downs that came from building a partnership and balancing the egos of two quite different people. Tony was a gentle soul. Mild mannered and cautious, he valued the simple pleasures in life, such as watching his beloved Fulham FC play on Saturday afternoon, catching up with the lads for a pint on Friday night and spending Sunday lunch with his family, which he did most weeks. He was a good, dutiful son, and I admired the close bond that he shared with his family, especially his mother who kept a tight ship and was adored by everyone. Tony wasn't particularly interested in climbing the corporate ladder, but he progressed up the ranks anyway. His success came naturally, as he was super-efficient and very likeable. His biggest extravagance was travel, and in the first few years of our marriage, when there was an abundance of money and time, we enjoyed lots of weekends away, mainly in Ireland, which was Tony's 'happy' place. I believe that we all have a happy place; somewhere where our spirit becomes alive and we glow with happiness that radiates from every cell in our body. My happy place is India, but Tony's was much closer to home. He loved the smell of the peat in the country air, the food (he could eat three bags of Tayto cheese and onion crisps in one go) and, of course, he loved his pint of Guinness. He'd spent every summer of his childhood with his cousins at Granny McNicholas's in County Mayo in the West of Ireland, and he talked fondly of those times. He was always melancholy when we left, and he held onto the dream of living back 'home' one day.

Aside from his melancholy when our holidays came to an end, there was also a deep, more permanent sadness within Tony. His son Nicholas was born out of wedlock when he was just 20, much to the disappointment of his parents who held very traditional views of marriage and family, and it took them a while to accept the situation, which caused him great pain. The relationship with Nicholas's mum fizzled out and they separated after two years. She remarried and took their son to Newcastle, which is a five-hour drive from London. Tony had a bitter fight on his hands to see his son, a fight that ate into his spirit and lasted for years. Tony wasn't a very open man, he was stubborn and tended to internalise his emotions. If he couldn't see a way around a problem he would just shut down. One ex-girlfriend used to call him the 'emotional refrigerator' because he just wasn't prepared to have those difficult conversations that we all need to have sometimes in life. When we argued, Tony could lock me out for days. He would ignore me, give me the cold shoulder and he rarely apologised first. It was his way, but it wasn't mine. I'm the complete opposite – I'm chatty and very open. I need to express myself and resolve a dispute quickly, with lots of talking and compromise. I believe our emotions have to be released otherwise they manifest into some form of pain or disease inside the body. But Tony held onto his pain, and I suspect all those years spent fighting to see his son left a deep scar on his heart, that beautiful, kind heart, which eventually gave up holding on.

As for me, what was I like back then? Well, I was pretty much the complete opposite to Tony. Where he was grounded, I was flighty, where he was a conformist, I was a maverick, where he was cautious, I was a risk taker, where he was practical, I was a dreamer, and where he was laidback, I ran on ambition. But for all our differences, we made it work. We had a foundation so strong in a love that we were both so grateful to find, and we had a shared passion for travel and socialising. These similarities far outweighed the differences in our approach to life.

We both loved to entertain, that's the Irish in us, and we regularly hosted parties at our house. Tony loved nothing more than to drink into the small hours and sing along with his booming pub voice to '80s classics. Music was his second passion in life, after Fulham FC, and Bruce Springsteen was his god. When Bruce went on tour, Tony would usually go to see his gig at least four times. He travelled all over the world to see The Boss, and when we got engaged I took him to see Bruce in New York. At seven months pregnant, my birthday present was to stand in the mosh pit at Wembley watching Bruce in concert again. I was a very accommodating wife and I didn't mind, well, not really! And I called in my one and only favour from my time working at the BBC to get Tony into an intimate concert in which Bruce played in front of just 300 guests at St Luke's Church in London. When he got to the door and realised he was on the guest list he phoned to thank me and cried his eyes out. I had just made a little boy's dream come true. So it almost goes without saying that music was a big part of Tony's life. He had a legendary vinyl and CD collection and he loved to spend hours making playlists for our parties. His music collection and Fulham programmes were his prized possessions. I bought him his precious iPod and a Bose docking station as a Christmas present the year we first met in 2002 and he was amazed at the little piece of technology that allowed him to carry his vast music collection around in his back pocket. He spent hours uploading his entire catalogue onto the player and arranging songs into amazing playlists for all our parties.

Our friends saw us as a beautiful power couple. We were two people who had found each other after a rocky start in life. We had an enviable lifestyle, fantastic careers and a beautiful home. To the outside world we had it all, but it wasn't enough for me. I wanted the family I had always dreamed of, with a mum, dad and two kids. I wanted another child. Initially, Tony wasn't so keen. His experience with Nick and the painful battle to see his son had left a deep scar on his heart, and he was happy with the family he had. He wasn't searching for anything else, but I was. I longed for another child to make my family complete and truth be known, I longed for another child to make *me* complete. There was something very primal within me that wanted, or rather needed, this second child, and if I'm honest I think it was to do with making amends for the child I didn't bring into the world when I was with Paul. But of course, you can't replace one child with another, and when beautiful Fionn came into the world on 7th August 2008, our hearts were filled with joy and I pushed the memory of my lost child into the wound that was buried deeply in my heart. I had my dream now: the husband, the family and the house. Life was complete. And Tony embraced fatherhood like no other man. He was inseparable from his little boy. From the moment I pushed Fionn out of my body, Fionn was in his father's arms and I barely got a look in.

We settled into domestic harmony, I took a year's maternity leave and loved being a mum and a housewife, and when I returned to work at the BBC we did our best to juggle our challenging jobs around childcare and family time. Tony's work frequently took him to Europe, which he didn't particularly enjoy as he preferred to be at home with us. He usually got the last flight home rather than stay over in some faceless corporate hotel, but he made an exception when he got the chance to stay in the Ritz Berlin! I don't think Tony could quite believe he had come that far in life to be staying in such a grand place. He still saw himself as a slightly awkward Irish boy from Southgate, London.

And so, life was good. Tony had just been promoted at work, we had finished rebuilding our beautiful home, his little boy Fionn filled his heart with unimaginable joy, and Fulham FC had got to the Champions League final – the first time in the club's history. And as for our relationship, well, that seemed to be turning a corner. We loved each other dearly but, as with most married couples, we had our ups and downs. I knew he loved me dearly but he had become a bit distant and withdrawn after our son was born. I put it down to the strains of having a new baby, the pressures of work and giving all his energy to renovating our house. We had a lot going on. I tried not to worry, and I prayed that it was just the flow of normal married life and that we would be back riding the crest of the wave again.

The night before Tony headed off to Scotland to start his walk was a run-of-the-mill evening. He returned home from work at 6pm and we ate dinner together round the kitchen table with my daughter Millie, who was 12 at the time, and our little boy Fionn, who was just 22-months old. I had a glass of wine but Tony never drank at home, he believed that it led people down the slippery road to alcohol dependency, and he watched me with a slightly disapproving eye as I topped up my glass. We let the pressures of the day slowly dissolve away and Tony focused his attention on Fionn, his precious little boy. The bond between father and son was fiercely strong. Tony was very involved in his son's life and when his daddy was around my wee little man didn't want to know me. In some ways I've always been grateful that I allowed them that space. It was almost as if Tony knew that his time with his beloved son was limited and he wanted to make the most of every moment he had.

After dinner I ran Fionn's bath and shouted for Tony to bring him upstairs. It was 7pm, and as I leaned over the banister I noticed Tony steadying himself on the console table at the bottom of the stairs. He had come over all dizzy and looked a bit greyish. When I expressed my concern, he assured me that he was fine. He was never really one to make a fuss, he just figured he'd got up too quickly and had a head spin. We thought nothing more of it and carried on the bedtime routine, with Tony putting Fionn to bed as he always did. Looking back at it now, I believe I had witnessed the moment my husband's fate was decided. It was the first of many 'signs' I was about to receive to prepare me for what was to come.

With the kids in bed we settled down to watch some TV. I had another glass of wine and we talked about Tony's forthcoming charity walk. I could tell he was excited, but nervous too. The Three Peaks Challenge is a real test of physical endurance, which involves climbing three of Britain's highest mountains in 24-hours. Tony had suffered from dreadful blisters during his training, which had refused to heal, so he was naturally concerned that his feet might not hold out. I wonder now if that was his only concern. I remember saying to him that he didn't have to do the walk, and that I would go in his place. It was no problem if he had to back out, but there was no way that Tony would admit failure – he was too stubborn for that. In hindsight (again), I realise that offering to take his place on the walk was not really a conventional thing to say, but I would have given my life for that man, such was my love for him, and after his death my suffering was so raw that at times I wished it could have been me in that grave and not him. I don't know whether it was his nervous energy or my subconscious mind propelling me into flight mode, but we ended up having a blistering row that evening and slept in separate rooms for the first time in our six years of marriage. We weren't the arguing types, but on the rare occasion that we did row it was usually a humdinger. But we'd never before resorted to separate beds; we had an unwritten rule that whatever issues we had with each other we would sort out before bed.

"Take care up those mountains,
I'm not ready to lose you just yet."

I sent that text to my husband at 9pm on Friday 25th June 2010, the night before he headed out to Ben Nevis on his charity walk. It was the last thing I said to him. I have no idea what guided me to use such words, as if it was my last chance to say I was sorry about our fight and that I loved him. You see, when you lose someone to a sudden death you look for meaning in that last moment of contact; those final words, that last look, what you were doing, how you felt, and I've since learned that people who are approaching death often retreat in some way, as if they are trying to create a protective barrier between themselves and their loved ones. Everything is more poignant when you are robbed of the chance to say goodbye. I don't remember the trigger for the argument, but I do remember Tony saying, "Dee, I hate you when you drink white wine, it changes you." And he was right, alcohol did change me. It turned me into someone whom I didn't like, someone who wasn't true to herself and was less compassionate and quicker to judge. But I just wasn't ready to hear that message back then, and over the years since Tony's death, as I've struggled with my grief and fought hard not to lose myself to drink, his last words have come back to haunt me.

The day Tony left for Scotland was not our best. He was still grumpy and angry with me over our argument the night before. He refused to entertain any conversation or small talk. He went into his shutdown mode but, despite his coldness, I tried to make amends and offered to help him with his last minute preparations and take him to the station. He refused my offers – he was stubborn to the end – but I'm grateful that I showed him this act of compassion. I know that in some ways I was just being true to myself and wanting to diffuse the unpleasant atmosphere – this was me to the core – but in another way I feel I was being protected. I can look back on what happened with a clear conscience, because I tried to bring us back to peace. I know I would have suffered unbearable regret and guilt had I not opened my heart and offered my help. So Tony headed off on his adventure and I went to a friend's for coffee. It was a beautiful summer's day and the children played in the garden as the gathering of mums chewed the fat and gossiped about their husbands. I told them all about Tony's trip and our argument. Then I said, "I hope he doesn't go and kill himself up those mountains, he'd be so embarrassed as he's hardly done any training." Those were my actual words, but nobody really paid any attention to my throw away remark. It wasn't until much later that my friend Elaine reminded me of what I said, as if somehow I could have known.

At 12pm on Saturday 26th June 2010, I received a knock at the door. There were two policemen standing there, and in that moment I knew. I knew that Tony was dead. I looked one of the officers in the eye and said, "It's Tony, isn't it?" and he nodded and replied, "Mrs Delaney, please can we come in?" I wouldn't let them in at first, I kept saying, "No, no, you can't come in, no." I didn't want them crossing my threshold with their bad news. I remember thinking that if I didn't let them in then maybe it would all go away, if I could keep it outside then perhaps it wouldn't be real. But there was no way to undo what had happened. Little Fionn was running up the hallway behind me all smiles, and Millie had come downstairs after hearing the door open. I led the two officers into the lounge in stunned silence and one of them opened his little notebook and delivered the facts: "Your husband was pronounced dead this morning at 9am, after having what appears to be a fatal heart attack," he said. "His body was taken by air ambulance to Stirling Mortuary. Here are the people you need to ring in the Scottish Highlands at the police station. They will be able to give you more details. We are very sorry for your loss, Mrs Delaney. Is there anyone we can call for you?"

I sat in silence for a while. I even offered them a cup of tea and joked that at least Tony had gotten to have a ride in a helicopter. And then, when the reality eventually penetrated my soul, I screamed that scream, that same guttural, heart-bursting scream that I'd heard Millie make the day I told her that her dad had died. It was a scream that united mother and daughter in pain forever. As she wrapped me in her arms to comfort me, Millie looked me in the eye and said: "Now you truly know, Mummy, now you know." And there was no denying that I knew.

When you're attached to another human being, as I was to Tony, and when that is taken away, it feels like everything is lost. What had gone was my identity, my place in the world, my whole life. I remember registering his death at the council offices and the lovely lady saying to me, "I'm sorry to tell you, Mrs Delaney, but you are no longer allowed to say you are married, you have to declare your status as widowed." And when she said that it felt so desperately cruel, like another loss. *I am no longer married.* I know it seems obvious, but at the time I just wasn't ready to accept that news. I was Tony's wife and now I was being forced to let go of a status that I had fought so hard to find. My journey to him and his journey to me had been a rocky path, but we had found each other and built a life that we both wanted. Now here was someone telling me that I couldn't have it anymore.

Well, screw you! I thought.

On the evening after the police's visit, everyone gathered round: my family, his family, our cousins, and our dearest friends. The shock and pain was unbearable. I remember phoning his poor mother with the news. She was driving and I heard her slam the car to a halt. She was simply inconsolable.

Her first words were, "What are we going to do, Dee?" and then, "How on earth am I going to tell Michael?" Tony's father, Michael, had been unwell for many years. My mother-in-law knew that the news would destroy him. We gathered in our grief later that day and went to our church to light candles. I was an active and practising Catholic at the time and needed to be close to my God. Our priest came to the house later that evening with his soft, gentle words of comfort, but in truth there was very little he could say to ease our pain.

The next day I flew up to Scotland with Tony's mother and brother to bring his body home. My mother, who lives in Ireland, flew over the moment she heard about Tony's death, and she looked after Millie and Fionn. Tony's father, who was unable to travel due to ill health, pleaded with me: "Dee, just bring my boy home, I need to see my boy." His pain was horrendous. In Ireland, it's commonplace to bury the dead within a few days – you die one day, you're in the ground the next. There are no endless hoops to jump through or mindless paperwork to fill in when someone dies. Compassion and commonsense prevail; you get the body in the ground and worry about the details later. In England, on the other hand, it can take between 7 and 21 days before a body is buried, but because Tony died in Scotland, under a different judicial system, I had to repatriate his body back to the UK first, so I was at the mercy of a whole lot of bureaucracy. I knew from previous conversations with Tony that he was passionately disapproving of the length of time it took to bury the dead in our country. He believed a body should be laid to rest within 24-hours, so in my heart I wanted to do this final act for him and get his body home and buried as quickly as possible.

Initially when we arrived at Luton Airport we were told our flight to Scotland had been cancelled due to technical problems and there were no other direct flights that day to the north of Scotland, where we needed to go. My spirit was broken. I needed to see my husband: to feel him, touch him, smell him. Tony's poor mum was distraught at this news too. She needed to see her boy as much as I needed to see my husband. He was mine, but he was also hers. I understood that. I was a mother too and I knew the bond she had with her son was as strong as the moment she pushed him out of her body. I could feel her pain as much as I could feel my own. I looked at her and said, with a fierce determination, "I will get you to Tony, I promise."

I grabbed the nearest airport assistant and begged her with everything I had to get us three seats to Scotland. And bless that beautiful angel; within the hour she had us on a flight to Glasgow. Once there we hired a car, drove through the mountains and got to the Highlands by Sunday night. As I went to bed that night I had a strong sense of Tony's spirit with me. I could see this white, cloudy shadow at the foot of the hotel bed. It was the outline of a person, and I knew it was my husband. I watched his presence for hours. I wasn't scared, but equally I wasn't brave enough to get out of bed and approach him. I talked to him and cried, "Why did you leave me? Why? I don't understand. I loved you, I loved you so much." And there I was laid bare with so many unanswered questions, but with 100% certainty that my husband's energy, his soul, his spirit, whatever it is that makes a human being more than just flesh and bones, had survived death. It was the bit that made Tony alive. My beloved husband was still with me in that hotel room in Inverness.

The next morning we went to see his body laid out on a slab in the hospital mortuary. The first thing I said was, "That's not my Tony, that's not my husband." And it wasn't. It was just the vehicle that Tony used for his spirit. Tony's body was parked there on the slab, but he had driven off on a new adventure. And I soon learnt that he hadn't gone far. In fact, he was at home in St Albans waiting for me. But first, I had to go through his belongings at the morgue, my heart breaking. And there I found a little piece of paper tucked inside his wallet, the same one I had given him with all my contact details on when we had first met. He had kept it with him every day as a reminder of that night, it was obvious that it was precious to him. I remember unfolding it, that tiny slip of paper represented the start of our story together, and here I was picking over the pieces from his dead body, with that bit of paper joining us at the beginning and at the end of our story.

We were due to stay another night in Inverness, but I couldn't bear to stay up in Scotland a moment longer, as I knew Tony wasn't there. I remember being in the hotel reception at 2pm after identifying his body, receiving his belongings and filling in endless forms. The paperwork that follows a person's death is mind blowing. It's as if we've created things to do to fill the void, because sitting in the void of grief is just too painful. I had his backpack on my back. It was the backpack he'd been wearing when he died. It was still stuffed with all his energy bars, drinks, plasters, and everything he thought he'd need to get him through the walk. I must have been a pitiful sight. The backpack swamped my tiny frame as I told the receptionist my story. With tears streaming down my face, I pleaded with her to get us three flights home that evening. There wasn't a dry eye in that hotel reception, but that amazing woman did it, she got us flights home that evening and my focus turned to getting my husband's body back home to St Albans as fast as I could. When the funeral directors told me it could take two weeks to get him back from Scotland I screamed, and I fought with everyone and everything that stood in my way to make it happen quicker. I was on a mission. This was my final act as his wife, and I'd promised his dad I would bring his boy home. I truly believe that when the will is strong enough anything is possible. And I did it. I made the impossible happen and got Tony home in six days. His body laid in rest in the funeral parlour for a further four days, to give us time to say our farewells. Each morning I would go up with his iPod, plug in his music and sing to him. The mornings were ours, and as I sang to his cold body, stroked his hand, rubbed his hair and willed him back to life, I thought how he had never looked so beautiful. He was at peace – I somehow knew that. After he died that iPod was like having a piece of Tony with me, and when I listened to the songs on it I was transported back to the happy times we shared together. Each song seemed to be laced with a special memory that captured a moment of our time together. It was incredibly powerful and in some ways I felt it was all I had left of him – he felt alive in the music. When I listen to his iPod today, his music always brings a smile to my face, but in those early days after his death his music helped me release an ocean of tears. In the evenings his family would attend his body. I'd kept my promise and Tony's father got the precious time he so wanted with his son. On the 10th day we said our final farewells, celebrating Tony's life in the way he would have wanted, at the Irish club in St Albans. We played his music, drank pints of Guinness and laughed and cried all at the same time.

And when everyone went back to the comfort of their lives, I stood still and looked into the void and cried. At night, when the stillness came, I watched as Tony's shadow danced around the walls trying to tell me, "Don't cry, Dee, it's all OK. I'm still here."

But I wasn't so open to Spirit in those early days. Understandably, my faith was shattered, and my heart was broken. I didn't know what to believe any more. Was it really Tony? Why wasn't he in heaven? Why was he here with me? I had so many unanswered questions. Then one morning, Fionn said to me, "Mummy, who is that man who comes to visit me every night?" I asked him what he meant and he said that there was a man by the window watching over him. I was stunned, *my little Fionn could see his dad's spirit too.* I told Fionn that I believed it was his daddy letting him know that he was always there and that he loved him very much. Fionn didn't question it.

Four years later, when my son was six, I asked if he remembered seeing his daddy at night. He replied, "Mummy, I can't remember but it must have been a shadow or a teddy. Maybe it was a ghost. But I know that if it was my father's love, then it is with me forever. His love travels with me wherever I am and never goes. Not just my father's, the love of everyone's family is always there. And sometimes Daddy's love is split for me and you. Mummy, I don't know anything about my daddy other than that he was alive. But I know he was a good man, that he died doing a good thing for charity, and that his love will be with me forever. And I know he will love you forever.

And so here I am now before you: a woman in her late 40s who has had two children, and a third child in Spirit with three different men who are no longer alive.

How can this be you might ask?
I've asked myself the same question time and time again.
All I know is that love is stronger than death,
And in the end death has led me to where I am now.
Death came to me as one of life's greatest teachers,
Death came to teach me about:
Anger and despair
Longing and lust
Guilt and shame
Death came to pull me apart and put me back together again,
And she also came to teach me about Love.
This is the story of how I came to be me,
The story of how I walked through the darkness to come out the Other Side.

PART TWO

A New Life Dawns

5

A Grief Laid Bare

"Grief is like the ocean, it comes in waves, ebbing and flowing. Sometimes the water is calm and sometimes it is overwhelming. All we can do is learn to swim."

Vicki Harrison

Grief is raw and unforgiving. It's ugly, indiscriminate, you never know when it's going to hit you and it feels like it will never go away. Well, that was my experience anyway, and I lived in the darkness of grief for five long years after Tony died. It was a lonely, miserable place to be.

In that first year after his death, I did everything to keep Tony alive. I just wasn't ready to let go. Life became one long round of ticking off events in his memory. There was his birthday, our anniversary, the annual summer party at our house. Every day, every week and every month there seemed to be some event or occasion that had a significance that didn't exist before Tony died. And as the date approached, I would start to feel the all too familiar surge of sadness consume my soul, forcing me to remember the happy times I had shared with my husband and exposing the enormity of my loss. It was easier in some ways not to remember, to block it all out, to not have to face the pain, but somehow these occasions sucked me back down memory lane and shone a spotlight on the life I'd had, the life I had loved, and the life I was missing. Grief is such an individual journey yet it goes through stages of acceptance, anger, denial and sorrow. I understood it all. I knew it was a process that I had to go through, but I never expected to feel so overwhelmed and paralysed by fear the whole time. I was literally frightened of everything and withdrew into myself, watching the world go by from the sidelines. Living with fear was utterly awful. It consumed me to the point that I didn't trust myself. Everyday decisions became a challenge and I felt incapable of doing the simplest of tasks. I actually felt removed from the world most of the time. I lived in a fog that separated me from reality. My body was stiff from self-medicating with alcohol, and I hated my existence. I couldn't bear to see families together and was jealous of their happiness. I noticed people looking at me and could sense them thinking, *there goes poor Dee and the kids, it's so sad.* Wherever we went the cloud of grief and our story came with us. I was like the fly in the ointment, spoiling other people's happy occasions with my sadness.

I started to put on the veil of survival about six months in, and I turned away from my suffering and became all philosophical about Tony's death, saying things like, "Well, at least he died instantly so he didn't suffer," and, "How honorable to die raising money for charity." I just didn't have the strength to sit with the pain, sadness and loneliness anymore. The only time I allowed myself to be sad was by his graveside. I went every single day for a year. I would spend hours crying my eyes out. I would talk to him and hug his headstone, and at times I lay down on the earth and pleaded with the ground to consume me and drag me into Tony's grave, such was my need to be physically close to him again. I didn't need to holdback my sorrow in the graveyard; it was the perfect stage for my tears. There is no need to put on a brave face when you're walking amongst the dead.

By year two I just wanted to run. I dug my heels in and said, "I'm not doing this anymore, it's too damn difficult." I was so unhappy and ANGRY, really bloody ANGRY. I questioned everything and everyone, failing to understand why I wasn't feeling better, and how I could still feel so heartbroken and wretched. I failed to accept my grief. I needed to observe it and understand that in time, as with all things, it would pass. But instead my grief turned into a form of self-hatred that had nothing to do with Tony's death, but had everything to do with me. I started to drink more than usual and became determined that life was to be lived now. I sold myself a line that I had to go out and meet someone else and have fun; I wanted a shortcut out of this bereavement. I was papering over the cracks, and I just brought more pain and suffering into my world. The first man I dated after Tony died was ravaged from hardened drinking. He was narcissistic, angry, deeply unpleasant and completely unfaithful. I knew from the first moment I met him that he was trouble. The relationship was very toxic and on two separate occasions complete strangers came up to me and said, "What on earth are you doing with that man?" I have no idea who sent these messengers to me, but I believe they were sent as a warning. I was pushing the self-destruct button with heavy drinking, and it was leading someone similar to my door. That's the way the world works, what you pay attention to will grow. My outside world was a reflection of my inner turmoil, and it wasn't pretty.

I've always had a love/hate relationship with alcohol. I grew up in an Irish community surrounded by drink, with a father who was never at home and spent everything we had on booze. In my 20s and 30s my life was a rollercoaster of working hard and playing hard. I was no different to most of my peers who liked to play, but I also knew that too much alcohol fuelled a lot of my negative behaviour. I remember being warned about the dangers of comfort drinking by a bereavement counsellor, who said it was easy to think that you are dealing with your grief by medicating the pain with alcohol, but grief doesn't work like that. Grief needs to be faced, felt and released – and the only way to do that is to face every dark, miserable emotion head on. Alcohol doesn't help you deal with your grief; it just gives you a drink problem to add to your worries. And of course, there was the matter of Tony's parting words the night before he died – "Dee, I hate you when you drink white wine, it changes you."

I was starting to see the full significance of those words now. It seemed that the universe was sending me a clear message. I needed to stop drinking and start dealing with my pain.

I soon realised that my relationships were becoming a powerful platform for learning. I dated someone else a year later who was teetotal, but a massive pothead. Different drug, same effect. He was completely uninterested in a lasting relationship with anything other than his joint. He dropped me like a sixpence after just two months. We're friends now, and he's in recovery with Narcotics Anonymous. I wish him so much love as he's a good man. He explained that he couldn't handle a relationship because he lived in a paradox of not wanting to be on his own but knowing that his smoking was holding him in a place of loneliness. His addiction kept him trapped in loneliness and I felt so sad for him, but I was also grateful for the lesson he was teaching me. He was showing me that I was no different, and that if I didn't bring my drinking into check, I too could easily isolate myself from happiness.

Those first few years without Tony were a very difficult time and I wasn't handling it well, and just when I thought I'd faced up to the worst of it the universe had something else up its sleeve. I was 39 when I conceived my son Fionn, and I loved being pregnant. I was one of those mothers who glowed, and I adored the process of watching my belly expand and feeling this new life growing inside me as I became more in tune with my body and Mother Nature. Pregnancy was always a time of great peace and connection for me. I had a perfectly normal and healthy pregnancy until I got to 29 weeks and my placenta ruptured and I started bleeding. This happened while I was gardening. As I pulled a weed from a flowerbed, I felt an instant tugging in my stomach. I remember holding my swollen belly and thinking, "Oh no, this isn't good." When I went to the toilet I noticed there was some spotting of blood in the pan and I called the hospital immediately. I was admitted for five days until the bleeding had subsided. Tony was playing golf in America with his best friend Ray when he got the call to say his wife was in hospital and to be prepared for the baby to come at any time. Poor Tony was beside himself and travelled for two days and nights to get to my bedside. While I was in hospital, I don't remember feeling particularly alarmed at any stage. I never suspected that my unborn baby could come to any harm – that just wasn't possible in my perfect world.

The doctors gave me steroids to support the baby's lungs in case I delivered early, and I was allowed home with the strict instruction to take it easy. Back in those days I didn't know what take it easy meant and within a week I was back at work, commuting for two hours a day and working for nine. I felt fit and healthy but my body was telling me otherwise. At 36 weeks, I had my second bleed and was signed off work for complete bed rest. This time I took the doctor's orders more seriously, although it still didn't register that my baby was in any danger. I knew many women who'd had bleeding throughout their pregnancies and had gone on to give birth to perfectly healthy babies.

By the time I got to 40 weeks, and was due to give birth to my son, I was put on high alert, strapped to a bed and surrounded by a team of medical professionals, who were all curious to see if I was going to bleed out during labour. It was a far cry from the natural home birth I'd desired. I was induced at 2pm on 7th August 2008 and fabulous Fionn flew into the world in record time, much to the surprise of everyone, including me! My labour was fast and furious. One minute I was in bed doing conscious breathing and riding the waves of contractions with ease, as Tony rubbed my back and read his *Empire* magazine, the next I was sitting on the toilet as my waters broke. The pan was filled with pints of blood and all hell broke loose. It seemed my ruptured placenta was more severe than first thought, and I was rushed to the delivery suite by the midwives, who screamed, "Don't push, don't push," as they took me up in the lift. The urge to push was so strong that all I could scream back was, "But I need to push, the baby is here!" We arrived in the delivery suite and three pushes later – at 6.36pm – Fionn took his first breath.

In the end, I was grateful to be in hospital. After delivering my son, the first thing I said was, "Oh my God, Tony, what's wrong with his eye?"

Fionn's right eye was all squashed up and I sensed in that first moment of seeing him that something was wrong. The midwives assured me that everything was fine, and that his eye was probably just full of all the goo from the birth. They cleaned him up and passed him to his daddy as I delivered my broken placenta and prayed that would be the end of it. But again, the nagging little voice inside me knew that it wasn't.

Fionn was a beautiful, angelic looking baby and was very placid and mild, easy to feed, a good sleeper and generally very chilled. He was and still is very content in his own world. He often stares into the distance, transfixed on whatever is 'out there', and he has a remarkable knowing that amazes me. And this knowing has revealed itself throughout the years in the little chats we've have just before bedtime or when he's having a quiet moment in the bath. There's something about Fionn's energy that almost draws you in. I feel completely safe in his presence, as if he's a much older and wiser soul than me, and I have always sensed that he was sent to guide me. His inner strength started to appear early on, when his cerebral palsy first came to light.

When Fionn was about two and a half, I started to become concerned about his physical health. As he approached most of his development milestones, I noticed that something wasn't quite right. He used to drag his right leg when he walked, and his core stability was weak which meant he struggled to pull himself up to standing. He was very uninterested in pursuing the usual physical activities of a toddler, such as climbing or cycling or running, and he never wanted to challenge himself, or even try. I put this down to the fact that we started renovating our house when he was nine months, and for the next year the place was basically a building site. As a result, Fionn spent most of his early days in my arms, as it wasn't safe to put him down on the floor. But as he grew older, his lack of physical strength was becoming more noticeable. He clung to me all the time and was very reluctant to try anything new. I wondered whether this was his own way of dealing with his daddy's death – he was just 22 months when Tony died, and, if I'm honest, with my own grief to deal with I barely had the energy to support myself, let alone nurture a toddler. So I hoped he might just come round in time, but this nagging feeling inside knew that something was not right. I asked my doctor to refer us to a pediatric centre, and we attended countless appointments with healthcare professionals and specialists who couldn't find anything wrong with him and treated me like a neurotic mother who was struggling because her husband had died. I was furious at the system, and tired at battling away when I knew something was wrong.

However, a physiotherapist who had been working with his mobility for over a year could also see something underlying and suggested that Fionn was presenting signs similar to someone with mild cerebral palsy. He had tightness in his lower limbs and was generally very floppy around his core, and he also struggled with his balance. I was completely stunned at the suggestion and went home and collapsed on the floor and cried on my own for hours. I knew something wasn't quite normal, but I just put it down to him reacting in his own little way to the loss of his father. But the enormity of what she was telling me was overwhelming. All I could think was, *First Tony and now my beautiful little boy might have a disability, what sort of godforsaken God could do this to me?* It was just too much to bear. I had never felt so alone. But this was something I had to face on my own, because in some ways I felt responsible for my little boy's condition. You see deep down inside I blamed myself for what happened in my pregnancy.

When Fionn was three and a half I took him to Great Ormond Street Hospital in London, where he had an MRI scan to see if he had suffered brain damage at birth. Because he was only a toddler he had to be sedated for the scan, which as any parent who has had to watch their child be sedated knows, is such a heart-churning experience. He struggled a lot in recovery after the procedure and kept screaming at me, "How could you let them do that to me, there is nothing wrong with me?" He's told me that same message many times over the years: "Mum, there is nothing wrong with me." You see, Fionn knows more about life and what it means to be whole and complete than I'll probably ever know, but at the time I was following medical convention and couldn't see life from the pure place where my beautiful son dwells. Fionn knows he's perfect, and he knows he's made in the image and likeness of God. He doesn't need you, me or anyone else telling him that there's something wrong with him, because that's not how he sees himself. He is a very content child in his own world.

But at the time, the brain scan told something different and showed that Fionn has periventricular leukomalacia (PVL), which is damage to the white matter brain tissue that is responsible for sending the nerve impulses that control motor function. The damage is usually caused by lack of blood flow to the foetus somewhere between 26 to 34 weeks of gestation. So, there it was. I was looking at a scan of my little boy's brain knowing that my actions that day in the garden caused damage to my son's brain which has left him with diplegic cerebral palsy. For me, this has been one of the hardest things to bear in life, beyond the pain of losing Tony, and it still makes my heart bleed. It feels like such a cruel lesson. Why should my little boy suffer the consequences of my impatience, my ridiculous need for a perfect garden, my stubborn determination to do everything myself – all those things that put me and my baby in harm's way in the garden that day? Why should beautiful little Fionn pay the price for my actions? And, somewhere deep inside, I hated myself for that one stupid act that will affect my son's life forever. It still makes my eyes well up with tears just.

I spent many moments wishing I could make his cerebral palsy go away. I was involved in a daily battle with him to wear the orthotic splints that held his heels down and wrapped round his ankles. He hated them with a passion because they slowed him down, were uncomfortable and made him different to the other kids at school. He gave up on them after two years. Then we moved onto night splints, designed to stretch his lower limbs while he slept. He cried every night as I struggled to get them on, saying they weren't snuggly and he couldn't sleep with them. He used to wake in the middle of the night, rip them off and fling them out of bed – they lasted a year. Then there was the daily physiotherapy which became a battle of wills, with him crying in pain for his daddy and screaming at me, "Daddy, daddy, I want my daddy," and, "Why do you want to hurt me?" The whole process has been exhaustingly tough, and all the while I've had this nagging finger poking me and saying, "You did this to him."

I spent endless days fighting and pushing against everything: his diagnosis, his physio, the constant appointments, but mostly my own pain at having to do it all on my own. It just felt so utterly unfair. And the reason it felt so unfair was that Fionn was a constant reminder of Tony, and the loss I was feeling deep inside. Every time I looked at him it was like looking into my broken heart. As for Fionn, other than the moments when he protested about the physio and wearing his splints, he accepted his body and grew up as a happy, beautiful and peaceful little boy. The fountain of love he has in his heart gives him the strength to be himself. I have never known a child to be so earnest and loving, gentle and kind. He truly is a child of God, and there have been many moments when he has wrapped his arms around me and comforted me in my times of need, just as I did when I was a child and consoled my mum through her sorrows. But I didn't want to be weak and vulnerable around my children. I didn't want to lean on them for support, but sometimes I had to accept that it was all I could do.

And as for me, well I know I tried my hardest at the time, but I also accept that I probably held Fionn back by trying to put him in a box that he didn't deserve to be in. By trying to protect him I was holding him down. In those early days as I came to terms with his physicality I kept making excuses for him, saying, "He can't do this because his legs aren't strong," or, "He can't do that because his balance isn't great." When all along what I needed to do was accept that my little boy is perfect as he is. I've had to dig deep to forgive myself for those early years of lack, where I was weak and couldn't muster up the strength to see beyond his little stiff legs and wobbly belly, and know that everything is possible if we believe in ourselves. My spirit was broken from grief, and Fionn's diagnosis was just another kick in the stomach. What I went through in those three short years, with Martyn's death, Tony's death and Fionn's cerebral palsy had virtually sent me over the edge, and little did I know there was more to come. But there will always be more to come, that's life. I have now learned that it is how we deal with life's ups and downs that makes all the difference. But I also now know deep down in my heart that there is so much to be grateful for. Fionn's cognitive skills are not affected at all, since his cerebral palsy is very mild. He is super smart, reads and writes very well and holds the most amazing conversations. He is emotionally very mature for his age, and he has the capacity to love that expands beyond anything I have ever known.

When he was six, we sat down together for the first time since his diagnosis, to discuss his cerebral palsy. I hugged him and said, "I'm so sorry, Fionn. I'm sorry for saying you can't do things, I'm sorry for not trusting that you know you are OK, and I'm sorry for all the boring physio. I promise I will make it fun from now on, and you have to start believing that you are perfect and can do anything you want."

And my beautiful boy hugged me and said, "It's OK, Mummy, you never knew me."

And then he said, "You never knew how important I was."

I looked at him stunned and he continued: "I have cerebral palsy and that's life. Some people have trouble writing. We all have something. It's OK."

That was the moment I knew the fight with cerebral palsy was over. I was going to embrace it, love it and everything it threw at me, because it's not separate from Fionn, it is a part of who he is. And if I'm going to love my son completely, I need to love his stiff legs and wobbly core and little eye squint and open my heart to all his perfectness.

6

Getting My Life Back

"When the spell of conditioning is broken, your Being dances like writing on water – spontaneous and untraceable"

Mooji

There seemed to be so much more wrapped up in how I was feeling than just my grief for Tony. His death was greater than my grief, it was the catalyst for change that moulded me into this new being that I am today. In some ways, Tony's death was my new beginning. It shone a spotlight on the dark corners of my life and forced me to ask some soul-searching questions about what it was I wanted for Dee. Everything was put into question and I took it as an opportunity to improve my life from the foundation up. My lasting memorial to Tony would be to be the best I could be in this world, the person I truly wanted to be and to find true happiness.

For the next five years, the process of coming to terms with my life and finding acceptance and peace with my story was, at times, torturous. But with the beauty of hindsight, I now know that Tony's death was the perfect parting gift from a man who adored me as much as I adored him. I have also learnt that this process to heal the self truly has no end. We only ever go deeper into ourselves when we truly learn to be at one with life. As I started to unravel, I began to realise that I had been brushing up against the real me throughout my life. But this being, who dances like water, was hidden behind all the conditioning that we humans pick up along the way. And although this 'being' showed herself many times as I was growing up, I was too blind to see. It was through my experiences with death that I saw with new eyes. My suffering and pain was like a gateway to a new world, and as I unravelled and put myself back together again, I discovered that there are no quick fixes, no places of perfection to aim for, and no end game. Life is in the journey. Our challenge, should we be willing to accept it, is to learn to let go of the reins and just let life be. But this was a challenge I struggled with for years.

"The ignorant strive to control life.
Life reveals itself to the wise."

Mooji

So, shortly after Tony died, I did what I always do when I'm faced with a crisis and started to read and research ways to deal with grief and heal my broken heart. My logical masculine mind needed to understand the process. I wanted in some way to transfer all responsibility for what was happening to others, to the experts. At the time I believed I had to look outside of myself for answers, that maybe by intellectualising the process I could make the pain go away. It was as much as I could do at the time to stay sane. I had always found Eastern philosophy particularly inspiring, so I read pretty much every enlightening book I could get my hands on, from *The Yoga Sutras of Patanjali* to *The Art of Happiness* by His Holiness the Dalai Lama, to *A Course in Miracles* by the Foundation for Inner Peace, and the New Age Bible *Be Here Now* by Ram Dass. I ensured that all bases, theologies and religions were covered! I also read books on bereavement. I remember this one book called *Living on the Seabed* by Lindsay Nicholson, a woman who lost her husband John to leukaemia at 35 and her elder daughter Ellie to the same disease shortly afterwards. I remember her story so vividly, especially how she described the pain of that time and how it took her eight long years to heal, move on and meet someone new. That fact stabbed me in the heart. Eight years felt like a lifetime to me. I couldn't possibly live in the fog of grief for eight insufferable years – I was too impatient. I knew it was her story, but something nagging inside me knew that it was partly mine, too, and I didn't want it to be. I didn't want to accept my life as it was, but I had started to identify with my victim story: the person who had lost Martyn then Tony, and then Paul. I kept thinking: *What have I done to create this reality? Did I somehow wish these deaths into being?* Lots of dark thoughts festered in my mind, and I was consumed with constant questions. I was sitting with a truth that didn't sit comfortably with me, and the truth regarded my grief. This was how it felt and I had to feel it. I had to ride the waves of grief, feel the tide ebb and flow, feel the pain and suffering, feel the calmness and rawness, to come out the other end. There was no short cut.

"Separated for eons
Or so it seems
I still remember YOU
The force that I forget
I always AM
And in this moment of recognition
I AM reawakened
To Being undivided"

Narayan

I often used to wonder what I would be like if Tony were still alive. I knew it was a pointless question, because I couldn't turn back the clock, but I had felt so utterly lost since his death. It's as if Tony took my soul and put a new one in its place. I no longer recognised the person in front of the mirror. I had identified so much with being Tony's wife, but that position was now redundant and I was left with this woman staring back at me who felt like she had no place in the world. I felt like one of those before and after pictures you see of people who have lost loads of weight. But although I weighed the same, I just didn't recognise who *I was*. I'd lost all sense of my SELF. And in truth, I had spent most of my life morphing into what other people wanted me to be. I was a people pleaser and I attached my sense of self to my status. I was a wife, mother, media guru, but these were just labels, things I did, functions I performed, roles I played, they weren't really who I was. I had always hidden behind the labels, but Tony's death unravelled me as a person and I questioned how I could move forward in life if I couldn't make sense of what it was that made me me. I no longer wanted to be labelled as a widow, or ascribed any other label for that matter, because I knew it came with a social currency that was meaningless. I had to break down a lot of my own value judgements about what was important in life, and I had to stop identifying with my story; be it my widow story, or my career story, because I became lost in the story rather than in living in the moment. I loved my time in the media; it helped fund my very nice middle-class lifestyle and brought me life-long friends who I admire and love, but, a year after Tony died, I made the choice to take myself off the conveyor belt and do something different. And it was a choice. I could so easily have stayed in the comfort of a solid career at the BBC, amongst colleagues and friends who would have supported me through my grief, but something inside me felt like I owed Tony more. I knew there was something else for me. The financial benefits that came from being widowed to an executive at a consulting firm meant that I could move on in life without worrying about money. But there was no sense of freedom, because freedom comes from being free on the inside, not free through financial or material means. I learnt that the hard way, and I would have traded every penny I had a hundred times over to have my husband back with me – but we can't undo what's done.

"They deem me mad because
I will not sell my days for gold,
And I deem them mad because
they think my days have a price."

Kahlil Gibran

So I took redundancy from my executive job at the BBC in 2011 and threw myself into practising and studying yoga. Yoga has, in many ways, been my lifesaver. The embrace of yoga kept me sane when my mind was troubled, and it allowed me to see grace when I felt so desperately sad. I developed a home yoga practice and turned up at my mat six days a week, even when on some days it was the last thing I wanted to do. I somehow knew I just had to show up. I found the physical asanas to be very grounding, and something inside me believed with 100%

certainty that yoga was the key to my healing. I always left my mat feeling lighter and more at peace than when I started, and that for me is where the magic is. It's in that feeling of stillness at the end of practice.

It was never my plan to teach yoga, but in November 2012, I ended up graduating from a teacher-training course in London and taught classes in and around St Albans. While I was on my training course I recalled a dream I had many years earlier, when Tony was still alive. I'm not one of those people who has what I'd call active dreams, where you clearly remember every detail in the morning. I am on the whole a very deep sleeper, but this visualisation/dream/premonition was very real and clear. In my dream I saw myself coming home from teaching an exercise class in the evening to a man who wasn't Tony. He was making me dinner, gave me a huge hug and was generally taking care of me. I couldn't see what this man looked like, but I knew we were romantically involved. I remember at the time thinking, *Well, I have no desire whatsoever to teach exercise classes and who is this man in my house?* But, 10 years later, in 2014, I walked into my boyfriend's house after my evening class teaching at a studio in Bushey and found that he had a big bubble bath waiting for me to jump into. He was also preparing our dinner. I remember telling him about my dream as I was curled up in his arms, and I had to acknowledge that I foresaw this special, shared moment. It was a moment of clarity amongst many that made me start to see the bigger picture. I was beginning to get a sense that I really had no control over my life, and that it is pretty much mapped out. It didn't scare me or bother me, but rather I had a deep sense of knowing that fascinated me. I believe that all the yoga and energy work had helped open me up to my inner self, and I was becoming more aware of this deep intuition that has always been there.

I gave a lot of myself when I taught yoga. I never once planned a class, I just showed up and gave my heart to whoever was there. I know my students loved my classes and my approach to practice was always deeply spiritual, but I found that teaching drained my energy and left me physically and emotionally depleted. I didn't feel as if I was teaching from a place of internal strength. I knew I needed yoga for me, and I gave myself to teaching because it is in my nature to help others, but there was always this nagging feeling that I was destined to do something else. This nagging feeling was my intuition, my inner guide, my truth calling me, but I had been so distanced from myself for so long that I was unable to feel it. I soon realised that this inner guide is the light that is always there, and it's been guiding me from the beginning. When I stopped and thought about my life it became clear to me that the most meaningful events in recent years were never actually planned – they just seemed to happen. I was starting to awaken. This process of opening to our intuition and inner truth cannot be controlled, rather it happens due to a sudden or gentle surrender to the knowledge that is already there. The truth is that everything we need to know is already inside us, and our intuition reveals this wisdom to us moment by moment when we get out of its way and stop trying to control life. We don't actually have to do anything to unlock the potential that is inside our hearts – the potential we were born with. But we get in its way through our human conditioning and our story. When we break the spell of our conditioning, we start to dance spontaneously in the stream of life, and that's when the magic happens.

"The very air I breathe
is given to me abundantly
the Life Force that makes my heart beat
is an offering to be renewed moment by moment
countless realizations of Truth
are presented in continuous flow
ultimately
I surrender
and accept love's invitation
to boundless life"

Narayan

In yoga we talk about this process of surrender as 'letting go'. For years I used to grimace in class when a teacher would say "just let go", because for me that had been the hardest thing to achieve in my practice, and in life. When we let go and soften into a pose, expansion and openness happens in the body and we feel the union of body and soul – we feel the magic. And it's the same in life. When we let go of the outcome and this human desire to control what happens to us, life flows with ease and magical things happen.

Today, my yoga practice remains precious to me, and I'm truly grateful for the blessings it has brought into my life, as it could so easily have gone the other way. Deep down inside, I knew it was either yoga or drink. At times it was both, but doing a headstand with a raging hangover is not to be recommended! Luckily, my passion for yoga helped me stay healthy and sober. You need a clean body to practice yoga, as it's physically demanding, and I noticed that when I had alcohol in my system my muscles were much stiffer and it was harder for me to access postures. But the more I practised yoga, the more my body craved clean foods. I stopped eating meat and followed an alkalising diet of green vegetable and fruits. I also reduced my alcohol intake to a minimum and now I'm healthier than I've ever been. For me, practising yoga has always been about healing the soul rather than getting into those pretzel moves and having a fit body. I never really push myself on the mat, as I like to feel calm and steady, but I'm always amazed when I achieve postures that I previously considered out of my reach. One of these is the Marichyasana D, an impossibly hard, twisty pose, which is described as a gateway posture in Ashtanga yoga because it necessitates broad opening in the shoulders, flexibility in the hips and grounding in the feet. I always avoided trying it because it just seemed hideously hard, which I know doesn't make sense, because how can I ever achieve a posture without practice? But, like most things in life, and yoga does reflect life, these things come to us in divine timing when we are ready. And in March 2015, I was ready. I achieved Marichyasana D when I came to a major crossroads and made a decision that changed my life forever. I chose to finally let go, follow my heart and hand over control to the divine inspiration in me, a higher being that I believe has a plan so vast and beautiful for me that I just have to trust and allow life to unfold, rather than trying to make things happen myself.

I came to this place because I had been trying for five years to fix everyone and everything in my path, but the truth was that it was never someone else that needed to change, it was me. My refusal to see inside my own heart had made me blinkered. It's easy to see the pattern now, with hindsight, but at the time I was living and breathing my painful widow story and bringing suffering to my door. Eventually I learnt to recognise that the patterns and programmes I saw in other people were the patterns and programmes I needed to heal in myself. It was the Law of Attraction presenting itself in all its glory. The Universal Law of Attraction states that we attract into our reality everything that we think and feel on the inside

– pure and simple. So if we live from a place of abundance, love, happiness and prosperity, we will send this energy out to the universe and receive it back. Call it karma, attraction, energy or like for like, what we give we get and what we reap we sow. If you send out love, abundance, happiness and prosperity, you get back love, abundance, happiness and prosperity. I knew and understood that, but my ego and analytical mind had been living in blamesville. In truth, my world was showing me a lot of pain, anger, guilt and sadness, and I knew that deep down it was the pain, anger, guilt and sadness in me that was voicing itself through the actions and behaviours of others. But, as we all know, it's a damn sight easier to turn the glare on others and blame them than to face the truth and accept that we are only ever responsible for ourselves. That's it. Nobody ever does anything to me; there is no 'out there'. There is only our inner world, which we project outwards, and all that we experience in life is a reflection of this inner self. I knew this deep down, and I also knew that I didn't like what I was seeing.

You see, I've spent the past five years stripping away at the meaning of everything, to the point where I believe that there are no coincidences. Therefore, if I manifest my own reality then I have to take responsibility for everything that has happened in my life, and that includes the things I don't like. It has taken a massive leap of faith to get to this truth. If I am ultimately responsible for all the ills in my life, then I must also have the power to correct them. And if the source of my reality comes from within me, then the source of my healing must also come from within. Life is that simple. It's what they describe so beautifully in the film *The Secret*. I know this belief is not for everyone, but my life's experiences have brought me to this place.

> *"Silence on the outside will lead to silence inside. That is why so many spiritual people observe 'silent time' for establishing contact with the Divine and charging their inner batteries"* [5]

So, on 21st March 2015, I stopped. I stopped everything and decided to just be. I gave myself the space to be still and to trust what came with the silence. I stopped teaching yoga, and gave myself a year off to just be. I set myself some broad rules of engagement. I wouldn't work, I would develop a consistent meditation practice, I would go with my heart, I would allow feelings to surface, I would look within for guidance and I would keep a journal. But I learnt quickly that you can't really have rules if you are just *being*, so I used them as signposts to bring me back to stillness when I veered off the path, which, of course, I did frequently. My heart knew that the path to my inner voice was through stillness. I kept filling the space with doing, and all the doing wasn't making me happy. I needed to sit with myself and ask the one simple question that I've been avoiding forever: "Dee, are you happy?" Yikes, how often in life do we sit down and ask ourselves this question? Am I happy? Go on, ask yourself the same question right now. Sit in front of a mirror, stare at yourself square in the eyes and ask yourself: Am I happy? Really ask yourself from the heart, it's scary, isn't it? Most of us can't even sit in front of the mirror, let alone ask the question. And if I'm honest, it's one of the hardest things I've ever done, but I was tired of running, and there was something greater than me guiding me to face up to my stuff, and to take a good hard look within. I knew it was just something I had to do. I gave myself a year. A year to do nothing and live in the flow.

And silence speaks.

When I finally allowed myself to open up and see the truth, I was astounded at what I discovered about myself, my children and my life's purpose.

PART THREE

My Healing Begins

Spring 2015

The 12 months that followed my decisions to stop, and just let things be, were the most expansive, magical and challenging of my life.

My soul had been craving a new way of being, and there seemed to be no escape from what life wanted to teach me. I was on a journey of personal discovery and there was no turning back. The only thing I knew for sure was that I was no longer in control.

The start of my journey in Spring 2015 was in some ways the hardest, but then I've often found the start of any project or adventure to be the most challenging time. I knew I wasn't going to be in for an easy ride, and I was scared of what I might find when I stopped and looked deep into my soul. During this period, I reflected on my childhood with such honesty and wholeness that I could see my true self for the first time.

What I saw was a little girl who desperately needed to be loved. A child who, through no fault of her own, blocked out the pain and suffering that came from growing up with a father who was a functioning alcoholic and a mother who struggled to deal with the life that had come her way. I realised I coped by trying to make things better for the family and by taking on the role of the 'good' girl. I was Little Lola, the girl with a bright smile who helped Mummy with all the chores and who tried to make everything better. I was the child who put everyone else first. In doing this, I denied my own feelings of sadness, anger and fear. I was the child who observed from the sidelines, who never complained for fear of upsetting others and who grew into a woman who became codependent on others for approval and love. I built a wall around my heart, suppressed my childhood pain and denied myself the greatest truth of all, the truth that 'life is suffering'.

This is the first noble truth from the teachings of the Buddha. I knew it well, but I couldn't see how it applied to me. It's a truth I denied from the age of three, when I refused to be addressed by my full name Dolores and insisted on being called Lola, Laura, Del, or, as I am now, Dee. Hearing the name 'Dolores' used to make the hairs on the back of my neck stand up. I remember physically cringing and disowning 'her'. But I never really knew why until that moment in March 2015 when I stopped and listened to her call.

The name Dolores means 'sorrows'. It comes from the Spanish Maria de los Dolores, meaning Mary of Sorrows, and it was traditionally given to the firstborn female in the family to represent the pain and suffering in childbirth. Little did I know that the answer to my life's struggles lay right there in my name! Suffering is part of life and only when we learn to accept the good with the bad, walk through our pain and feel our fear can we truly begin to grow as a person and start our journey towards peace.

The concept that life is suffering is best explained in the opening lines of the book *The Road Less Travelled* by M. Scott Peck.[6]

Life is difficult.
This is a great truth, one of the greatest. It is a great truth because once we truly see this truth, we transcend it. Once we truly know that life is difficult – once we truly understand and accept it – then life is no longer difficult. Because once it is accepted, the fact that life is difficult no longer matters.

Over the years I created a blind spot regarding my negative emotions and chose only to see the good in life. By doing this I created a world with a false reality. This was a world in which I associated love with pain and replayed the emotions and feelings I'd denied since childhood in my adult relationships. I was in a cycle of deep denial and it was playing out as control:

control of others, control of myself and control of life. I had lost myself in the name of helping others and the universe was trying to teach me another way. I was so disconnected from the full spectrum of human emotions that it was as if I had denied a part of me existed. This was my 'shadow side', as the Swiss psychotherapist Carl Jung describes it. It was the part of me I didn't want to see – the negative part that had been causing havoc in my life but was also calling out to be heard. This was the part of me that was lost.

So I stopped and I listened. I took those first nervous steps on 21st March 2015 – the sixth anniversary of Martyn, my daughter's father's, death. The date was no coincidence. The universe saw it as an opening for my soul to awaken. It was a time to reflect on my outer life – my relationship with Martyn and the lessons he had taught me. This was springtime, when the earth is coming out of darkness and into light. It's a time that symbolises new beginnings and creative expression and provides an opportunity to access the healing energies of Mother Nature. It was a time for change and during these three months the universe taught me some important lessons:

- ***To move forward in life we need to understand and forgive the past***. When we accept feelings and emotions from our childhood that are buried deep in our unconscious mind we bring them into conscious mind and allow them to heal.

- ***We need to accept suffering as part of life.*** There is no light without darkness and no joy without pain. Life is a balance of opposites and to deny one part is to deny the other.

- ***We are only ever responsible for our own lives.*** When we take responsibility for our world, the world around us changes. In the words of Mahatma Gandhi, "You must be the change you wish to see in the world."

- ***Life keeps on giving.*** The universe never gives up on you, even if you keep repeating the same mistake time and time again. The lessons continue to come until the soul finds meaning and evolves. Our free will decides when that lesson is received.

7

Accepting What Is

"Nobody ever told me that grief feels so much like fear. I am not afraid but the sensation is like being afraid. The same fluttering in the stomach, the same restlessness, the yawning. I keep on swallowing." [7]

This is how I felt on that morning in March 2015, when I arrived back home from the school run with heaviness in my heart and an unexplainable sense of trepidation. I knew I was about to go to a place deep inside me that I had been avoiding my whole life. I was grieving, not for my late husband, but for me. And as I walked into the living room and glanced around at the trappings of my comfortable middle-class existence, I felt only emptiness inside. None of it mattered. I was sitting in my beautiful home in St Albans, where I'd always dreamed of living, but I was dead inside. I felt nothing, just this vacuum of space that was disconnected from anything real. The stillness was suffocating, but I sat with it anyway, I was done running. I knew I just had to sit out this moment of discomfort, and then the next moment and the one after that. I had to sit in the stillness and accept what came. I focused on my breath. Years of yoga practice had taught me that the breath is the gateway to the inner self, so if I could just get past the panic and anxiety and get through the veil between my internal and external experiences, I knew I would get to the other side, to the realm of the soul. The veil is where the battle of the will happens. It's what holds on to the secrets and hurts and suffering of the past and it's what I needed to pass through to reach the timeless stillness of the light within me.

I held this place of stillness for the briefest of seconds and invited a flood of emotions to the surface, releasing with it a torrent of tears I'd been fighting for years. At first, I tried my hardest to stifle the sobs and push them away. My lifelong habit of denial wanted to spare me the suffering and pain. But somehow I finally found the strength to give up the fight and surrender. I stopped trying so damn hard to make everything OK. I stopped putting on the veil and for the first time in years I started to feel. An unexpected avalanche of unstoppable tears rolled freely down my cheeks, saturating my neck and wetting my clothes. And although I had cried a thousand tears for my husband Tony when he'd died, these tears were different. These tears were for me. They were tears for the little girl inside me who I'd denied for so long, and who wanted so desperately to be heard. And, as I closed my eyes, I could see a little girl right in front of me. She had pigtails and a bluntly cut fringe that emphasised a pretty, cherub-like face. She felt so real it was as if I'd travelled back in time and gone into my childhood body. I could see the sadness in my eyes and, as I was drawn in by the image of my childhood self, I held my arms out to give her a cuddle. But she wasn't 'out there,' she was deep within me.

"Oh my God, it's me, it's me, it's me," I cried. I wanted to cuddle her and tell her everything would be OK. And, as this realisation dawned on me, my arms naturally found their way round my shoulders and I gave myself a loving, nurturing embrace.

"It's OK, little Lola," I whispered. "I am with you now."

The whole experience felt raw and so very painful. It hurt to know I'd denied all these feelings for so many years and had lived behind an impenetrable façade, one that was now showing signs of cracking and allowing the light of truth to shine through. But as I nurtured my child within and told her how much I loved her, I also experienced a beautiful moment of deep healing. And that really was the moment my life changed forever. I made the choice then to stop running and to start healing.

"Whatever inner worlds I choose to explore
or how subtle and etheric my sensations may become

no matter how far over time and space I travel in order to heal
I AM going nowhere, and nothing is coming to me
in this silent celebration of unity"

Narayan

I started to see how my childhood experience had influenced the behaviours and patterns in my adult life. I started to 'own' my childhood story, not from a position of blame, through pointing the finger at my parents and saying, "You did this to me", but from a place of oneness that saw my mum and dad as two people; two souls on their own journey who were doing the best they could. I stopped judging my parents and turned the lens on me. Judgement is another form of control. When we judge we give advice and opinions, but when we empathise we listen with an open, knowing heart. Acceptance is the antithesis of denial and control, but it comes from a place of non-judgement, where you can allow things to be without the need to change them, even if that feels sad, frightening or overwhelming. When I let go of the controls and stopped judging, I began to see my childhood stories through new eyes of awareness. I started to 'parent' my own inner child from a place of love. I would sit in meditation with her each day and conjure up the little girl with pigtails. As I gave her the space to come forward, the love I sent her allowed the pain and suffering that I had held onto for years to rise to the surface to be healed. I realised that through the openness of my heart, I could literally reach the sadness from my childhood that was stored in my body and shine the light of love on it. As I did this, I felt the energy of the stored emotions rise throughout my whole body and dissipate out through my ears. I was letting go. I was transmuting the suffering and pain that I had held onto from my childhood story into love. And if I can do this, so can you. By sitting with myself in silence and going into the pain, I was healing myself and making peace with my story.

When we are young children, most of us think Mummy and Daddy are the perfect female and male archetypes and we believe everything they say, thinking they can do no wrong. And while it is every child's basic right to be loved and nurtured, not every child is fortunate enough to experience this. When a child grows up in an environment where their basic needs aren't met (by one or both parents), they will find other ways to compensate for this 'lost' love. And more often than not, they will believe they did something wrong – because in their eyes Mummy and Daddy are perfect. And this is just how it was for me. Instead of seeing my father's failings as his own and expressing this loss through tears, sadness or anger, I turned the finger of blame on myself. I questioned why I wasn't good enough and wondered what I could do to gain his love. I suppressed my feelings and did everything I could to try to fix the *situation* and make my daddy love me. I became the good girl in the family: the strong one who looked after my mum when she wasn't coping. I cleaned the house and from the age of 14 I even did Dad's business accounts. I did everything possible to try to make things better, but I couldn't control my dad's life. His life was for him and him alone.

"Expectation is the mother of frustration, but
acceptance is the mother of peace and joy." [8]

Over time, my relationship with Dad improved. As he became more involved in my life, we developed a special closeness. I stopped judging him for being an absent father and started to accept him for the man he was, faults and all. He cried as he walked me down the aisle when I married Tony and helped me renovate my house in St Albans. He knew how much I wanted to settle down and have a place I could finally call my own and it was his way of saying sorry. He also cheered with pride as he watched me collect my master's degree and he was the first person to come to my side when Tony died, picking me up off the floor and holding me in his arms as I sobbed over the sheer enormity of my loss. My children held a special place in his heart, too. He used to take Millie and me for days out when I was a single mum and hated being on my own. After Tony's death he came around every Saturday to kick a ball with Fionn. And, although he was still fond of the drink, he also found happiness when he allowed a beautiful soul called Betty into his life. She became his life partner and accepted and loved him just as he was. She gave him a second chance of having the family life that maybe he wanted as a young man, but hadn't been able to accept. I will always be eternally grateful to Betty for the love and compassion she showed my dad. She was by his side for 20 years, right until the end.

Dad left this world on 26th April 2012, surrounded by the loving embrace of Betty and his four children. Being there as he took his final breath was probably one of the most serene experiences of my life. I rested my hands on his feet and felt his life force move up through his body as he took those last few steps home. For a moment I felt as if I was in the presence of God, and I knew in my heart that Dad was finally at peace.

In his book, *On Becoming a Person*, Carl R. Rogers writes about acceptance when he says, "*The curious paradox is that when I accept myself as I am, then I change…we cannot move away from what we are, until we thoroughly accept what we are.*"

As we develop in life, we are very much guided by the world we create around us. This world is influenced by many *views*: our internal view, our family view, our worldview and our cultural view. Our internal view is how we see ourselves – it is the lens on our inner self that tells us we are loved, secure, and wanted. But it is also the inner voice and critic that tells us we are naughty, worthless or lazy. Our sense of self-worth and how we value ourselves is directly related to the feeling of being valued by our parents. The quality of parental care we receive as children is fundamentally important if we are to progress into adulthood with a deep sense of internal love and security. Children who receive constant nurturing and love grow up to be adults who have a deep internal sense of their own value and security. But those who are denied consistent care and nurturing by one or both parents in childhood grow up with a sense of lack. They feel abandoned, fear the future and tend to look outside of themselves for the love that is lacking on the inside. As I reflected on my childhood experience and my life, I could clearly see I was one of those people. I began to realise that my constant search for peace and happiness was to do with the fact I carried deep wounds from my childhood, which I had kept buried for years. And my story showed itself through my body, as it does for everyone. The body is the vehicle for the soul, and each body tells its own story.

Experienced cranial osteopaths can tune into a body and read its story, pinpointing past traumas or blockages carried in the bones, ligaments, fascia and spinal fluid of their clients. They can relay these stories back to their clients without them even opening their mouths! It's fascinating work. And with most things in life, it's often easier to see these bodily characteristics in others than it is in ourselves. For instance, when we see someone whose shoulders are up around their ears we know it's because they are highly stressed. Or we might be able to figure out that someone who is heavy set is this way because they've fed their emotions with food rather than dealing with them. Or, at the opposite end of the scale, that someone who is hyperactive and thin is this way because they've lived on their nerves.

Learning to become more body aware has been an essential part of my healing. Our generation might well be progressive in terms of technological advancements and global connectivity, but the truth is we are much less connected to ourselves than our ancestors were. This is because technology has cut us off from the source of true power, which comes from nature and the inner wisdom that lives in every cell and tissue of our body. Practices like yoga and meditation help bring more awareness to the body, as they teach us to direct the breath and mind to the part of the body that is calling for attention. And as I've said before, the body is merely a vehicle for the soul so when we learn to listen to our bodies we are actually tuning into our higher selves.

I only started to become more body aware after five years of daily yoga practice. I'm at the point now where if I am carrying any tension or stress, I can sense it on an energetic level and so I ask my body what it needs from me. For instance, when I feel burdened by responsibilities this usually manifests as a niggling pain in the back of my right shoulder blade. When this happens, I know it's a call for me to look at a situation and make changes in my life. Once I've implemented this, the pain automatically goes away.

I also began to notice that I have a childlike body and girlish voice, which is slightly unusual for a woman my age. Also, I naturally stand with my hips swaying forward and my chest sunken in. I've stood like this since my teenage years. When I look back at photos of myself, I can clearly see my belly sticking out because of the position of my hips. And my shoulders are rounded as if I am trying to protect my heart and close in on myself. It's as if I've always been fighting against my body.

During yoga practice, I advance quickly with some postures but remain stuck on others. Luckily, my curiosity to learn more led me to an amazing book called *Eastern Body, Western Mind* by Anodea Judith[9]. This taught me about character structures and gave me the answers my body has been trying to show me for years. I always knew the right books would come to me at the right time, and this was one of them. It presents a pathway to healing by integrating the Eastern philosophical system of chakras with Western psychology. In some ways, I felt the book mirrored my life.

In 2015, I was 46 – that's halfway through my life, if I'm lucky enough to live to a ripe old age – and I was at a crossroads. I was consolidating all the knowledge I had gained from around me: everything I had learnt from my spiritual practice, through therapy and through my new understanding of the psychological and emotional challenges I faced in my childhood. I was merging my Eastern side and my Western

Side. I was at the heart of these two sides of my being. And this awakening was instrumental in helping me integrate all parts of my being at the physical heart, which is the centre of the universe. And when we truly live from this heart space we become open to the oneness of life and start to see the world from a much higher level of consciousness. A place of unity consciousness within , a place of love. This was where life was leading me.

"When I see you with an open heart
my heart is opened further
into a unified field
where hate melts into love
and love is oneness
uncreated"

Narayan

When we experience difficulties during key development stages of our life, we develop coping strategies to protect ourselves. In effect, we put on our *armour* and go out to either fight the world or withdraw. This *body armour* is locked into our tissues and reveals itself in our posture and through distinctive characteristics. Bioenergetics, as pioneered by the American psychotherapist, Alexander Lowen, uses the language of the body to heal the problems of the mind. His works prescribe six typical body armours that the individual can identify with:

A: *The Creative/Schizoid* has a typically tall and lean body shape, and appears to live on their nerves. People with this structure overly intellectualise their existence, and their creativity feeds their right to exist, which was challenged by their mother's lack of bonding in the womb and in early childhood.

B: *The Oral/Lover* typically has hips that sway forward and a sunken chest. They tend to either be very small or very large. Orals want to merge with others and are people pleasers. They can be needy and have addictive personalities. They also fixate on others.

C: *The Masochist/Endurer* is typically thickset around the middle and has a dense, heavy body. They hold everything inside and become stuck in cycles of pleasing and resisting, which develops normally as a result of an over-controlling parent. They live in terrible conflict with themselves because they hold everything inside and fear being exposed to their true feelings.

D: *The Rigid/Achiever* is typically a good looking, athletic and high achieving man who lives in the persona of a perfect world, but is very disconnected from the inner self. This characteristic develops at the age of four to seven, when the parent withdraws from the child and expects them to grow up. In turn the child's vulnerabilities and weaknesses are not nurtured. This creates issues with commitment and fears around intimacy in adulthood.

E: *The Hysteric* is typically a pear-shaped woman, with a small upper body and large hips and thighs. They are overly emotional and crave attention, and this characteristic develops when the father lacks empathy as the child matures and the expectation for achievement is high.

F: *The Challenger/Defender* typically has broad shoulders, narrow hips and a strong physical presence, with a confidence that masks their insecurities. They have a tendency to attack and defend as a result of their own vulnerabilities, which were seen as a weakness by their parents at a time when they were seeking autonomy. As a result, they must win at all times.

Each character type carries some kind of deficiency or excess somewhere along the chakra system, which is an Eastern philosophical model for life. As we develop, we move through each chakra and expand our state of consciousness. What this means in simple language is that we bring more meaning, compassion and understanding into our existence. As we integrate the individual with the divine wisdom of the universe, we learn to live from a place of true empathy and love. Yoga is one of the key disciplines that helps us to work on the chakra system. There are seven main chakras and these run from the base of the spine to the top of the head. Their function is to receive, process and express life force or energy.

"Chakras are not physical entities in and of themselves. Like feelings or ideas, they cannot be held like a physical object, yet they have a strong effect upon the body as they express the embodiment of spiritual energy on the physical plane. Chakra patterns are programmed deep in the core of the mind-body interface and have a strong relationship with our physical function." [10]

By looking at the body and examining our habits, we begin to see the patterns we use to deal with stress or trauma. Most people tend to either avoid situations or overcompensate when faced with difficulties. Different character structures appear as a result of our excess or deficient coping strategies throughout key development stages. Take a look at the descriptions above and see which character best describes you and your story. I could easily identify myself and my story with the Oral/Lover body armour. In fact the description, nearly flew off the page and I had one of those enlightening OMG moments , jumping up and down and screaming, that's me, I am textbook Oral.

Oral Characters, like myself, are known as the *undernourished child.* They suffer from emotional wounds and desperately want to be loved. When they struggle to find this love they find comfort around food and other oral activities, such as excessive talking, smoking or drinking, etc. They have difficulty forming boundaries, believe that love will solve everything, feel empty and abandoned and have a deep fear of letting go. Oral characters are deficient in the first chakra, whose Sanskrit name is Muladhara, meaning 'root support'. (I will talk about the development of other chakras throughout the book.) The first chakra supports the basic need for survival, safety, nourishment and physical health. It correlates with the development stages from the womb to 12 months and the concerns of trust, stability, prosperity and good health. It represents our physical reality, our relationship to the body and the world around us. The root chakra connects us to Mother Earth, our physical mother and our ability to mother ourselves and others. In yoga, a balanced first chakra is achieved through grounding via the feet and legs. Grounding refers to the connection between the soul and Mother Nature. When a person is grounded, the soul is centred within the body and the body has a strong connection to the earth, which brings a feeling of strength, vitality and balance. This connection comes from drawing energy up from the earth through the feet and along the spinal cord. When a person isn't grounded, they usually feel anxious, fearful and unprotected by the earth. Throughout all my years of yoga practice, I have always struggled to ground my feet. My heels always want to rise off the mat or my toes seem to grip on for dear life. But, as I explained before, the body never lies, and what we feel and how we present ourselves in a posture is always a reflection of our inner soul. And it seems my feet have been trying to tell me something for years. They were asking me to draw deeper into my roots and reclaim my childhood.

I started to do this by actively grounding myself in my yoga practice. I brought new focus to my feet and really concentrated on my foundation in each posture. I also spent a lot more time outside in nature, in the ground. I stood barefoot on the grass in my back garden every day for 10 minutes and visualised roots from my feet travelling deep into Mother Earth and drawing vital energy up into my body. As I took a deep breath in, I imagined this energy of Mother Earth as a golden orb of light drawing up through my feet and feeding my entire body and I felt myself become strong and expansive. As I breathed out, I pressed my heels firmly down into the grass and released any stress or worries that I was holding onto into the core of the ground. This helped my body become freer and lighter. Other techniques you can try include gardening with bare hands, walking in nature, receiving a massage, taking a shower to wash away any negative thoughts or moisturising your body. Eating root vegetables and heavier foods like pasta can weigh you down and keep your feet firmly on the ground.

"The wound is the place where light enters you."

Rumi

As I actively started to draw deeper into my childhood story, and my ground, I began to develop a lot more compassion for my mother. I realised how in some ways I was repeating the same story in my intimate relationships as she had with my dad. As I connected more deeply with my mum we started to talk about the past and her life growing up in Southern Ireland. History has a way of repeating itself, and the wounds of our parents and ancestors travel down through the family line. The physical and emotional traits present themselves from one generation to the next, so when we understand our parents' story we can move from a place of blame to one of empathy, bringing healing and awareness to the physical body and changing the negative patterns and behaviours that affect our lives. If you get a chance, sit down with one or both of your parents, or a close relative from the same generation, and ask them to tell you their story. What was life like when they grew up? Did they have money issues? Was there enough food? What bonding and nurturing came from their mother and father? What was their diet like? Did they experience a childhood illness? Were there major traumas in the family, such as deaths or threats to survival, etc.? Everything is connected. What I learnt from talking to Mum was that we shared the same story of loss and abandonment; hers was for her father, mine was for my dad. Talking to Mum really helped to shine a light on the deep emotional wounds of the soul that I was being called to heal. We are often unaware of these soul wounds, but they come to us through behaviours and repeated patterns that occur in our lives. My ability to constantly attract men just like my dad – men with alcohol issues – was feeding my wound of abandonment. This wound affected my mother, my grandmother and my great-grandmother. It had woven its presence through my ancestral lineage, and the energy of abandonment was feeding its way through my bloodline. I began to appreciate that far from being weak, my mother was actually very strong to stay in a relationship that made her so unhappy. Because when faced with abandonment, the typical reaction is to run away, which is how, up until now, I had dealt with it. I would find every conceivable way to push away whatever it was that triggered the deep-seated feelings of grief, anger, despair and frustration from the depths of my soul, rather than face the issues that lay under the wound. To stay is to go beyond the darkness and into the Shadow Self, which I talk about in the following chapter. To stay is to dare to look into our own darkness and the collective shadow of our ancestors. It is here that we learn the most potent lesson from abandonment, which is the art of polarities, and how we cannot be one without the other. And through it we come to understand that to have been abandoned means we are capable of abandoning, which is what I had been doing all my life – abandoning mySelf in order to please others. We come to realise there can be no love without grief, no dark without light. And when we get to the roots of our abandonment and start to face ourselves, as I did when I hugged my inner child, we start to unravel and bring understanding, clarity and transformation into every aspect of our lives. And through it all I have come to have deep gratitude for the woman who gave me the gift of life. For my mum stayed through the pain and suffering out of love for her children, when she could have so easily run. And I now understand that my parents were my greatest teachers, and I 'chose' them so that I could learn the lessons that life wanted to teach me. These lessons haven't been easy, but without them I wouldn't be who I am today.

8

Denying What Is

"Beware of the posture of pretence of 'helping' others
It may be nothing more than a masked avoidance in facing
one's own misconceptions born of a deluded mind."

Mooji

I believe people come into our lives for a reason, and my first great love affair after Tony died was with The Big Guy[11], who came into my life to teach me about duality and polarity and how to confront the problem of opposites in human nature.

I met The Big Guy in March 2014, after being introduced by a mutual friend. Our physical difference was the first obvious opposite. He's a big, burly giant of a man, standing well over 6ft tall and is heavy set like a big bear, whereas I am 5ft31/2 inches – that extra half inch makes all the difference! I'm slim and tiny in comparison. My body and voice are almost childlike, which is typical of the Oral character structure I discussed in the previous chapter. The Big Guy, on the other hand, is a classic Masochist/Endurer character[12] structure, with a dense, heavy and muscular body. And true to his character type, he has a tendency to hold his emotions in, whereas I am dependent and clingy. The Big Guy was the boyfriend I talked about in the beginning of the book who appeared to me in an apparition when I was teaching yoga. He was the first man I ever connected to on a deep soul level, and our relationship has been so intensely transformational that at times we have both wondered what on earth was going on. We couldn't explain the strength of our connection, other than it felt as if something greater than ourselves was pulling us together. This force was so strong that The Big Guy would sometimes vibrate when I touched him. We were like magnetics. And like magnets, our opposite traits pulled us together while our similar ones pulled us apart. The Big Guy possessed all the traits I failed to see in myself, and I had the ones he failed to acknowledge in himself. For example, where I showed strength he showed vulnerability, where I was disciplined he was undisciplined, where I was serious he was great fun, and where I was angry he was contained. I was living a very one-sided life at the time. My friend Jennifer described me perfectly when she called me the Christmas Fairy. I had my head and heart in the clouds, and I sprinkled peace, love and happiness on the world around me. And when it came to my relationship with The Big Guy, there was a lot of giving and not much receiving. I felt constantly drained, as if he was sucking the life out of me. I literally gave everything to that relationship, but I gave from a place that was lacking. I was half empty and broken inside, and I was lacking the wholeness you need to give to another.

And The Big Guy was broken too. Divorced for two years, he was stuck in the past, pining for the lifestyle he had with his glamorous ex-wife. He found it hard to accept the separation from his 8-year-old daughter, who he missed dreadfully and lived for the weekends when she visited, and was lost in a fog of depression and drink when she wasn't around. And I thought I could fix him. You see, for someone like me, someone who has been all about trying to fix others, The Big Guy was my perfect match. He was needy, lonely and sad and I needed someone who was needy, lonely and sad to distract me from my own pain. I needed the distraction of someone else's drama to deflect me away from dealing with my own issues. And The Big Guy was the perfect guise. I remember our initial meeting in a bar in St Albans. When I first set eyes on him I felt a stab in the pit of my stomach. This told me 'this guy is trouble' and I needed to run. It was the red flags of my intuition screaming at me that this wasn't going to be a healthy relationship. But some other '*part of me*' was curious and wanted to go on the ride anyway. So I did. I entered a year-long relationship with The Big Guy that felt like I was travelling through a thousand years of pain, suffering, joy and love all rolled into one. I have never been so consumed, so lost or so obsessed by someone before. At times I felt like I was going insane, and at other times I felt such blissful contentment I thought I had died and gone to heaven. And The Big Guy felt the same. But ours was a love affair involving two people who desperately needed to heal. The Big Guy was an alcoholic in denial and I was a codependent in denial. To the outside world, I was a sweet, loving yogi, but inside I was dreadfully lost and unhappy and I didn't understand why. Tony had been dead for four years and I generally felt I had done the work and grieved for him in a full and honest way. I hadn't shied away from my pain, anger or loneliness. I had felt every knock and bump along the path of grief, but my heart was still broken.

So, in the first flushes of this new relationship, I thought I had finally found the happy ever after I had been searching for since Tony's sudden death. Had I learned nothing?

We did have a lot of fun in those early days, The Big Guy wined and dined me, brought me beautiful flowers and expensive gifts and treated me like a queen. I genuinely thought I'd hit the jackpot. There was lots of partying and way too much drinking, which I never questioned even though I knew he had been to rehab. In my naivety and desperate need to escape my loneliness, I chose to ignore the obvious and enjoyed the escapism. In just a few short months we developed a deep bond and mutual respect for each other. The Big Guy became my lover, my confidant and my best friend. I felt like I could open up and tell him everything, and by doing so he got to see the real me. I didn't have to hide behind the mask with him – he got the full, unedited version. He listened to me laugh and cry and he watched me scream with anger and dance around the living room full of joy. He saw it all. And he never once judged me. He sat, listened, comforted and pretty much accepted me just as I was. We used to spend hours talking on the phone in the evenings, filling the emptiness in our hearts with constant chatter. We had a lot to talk about, as we both understood what it was like to grow up in a family with an alcoholic father. Our dads actually knew each other, they used to drink in the same pubs back in the heyday of the '70s and '80s. We suffered the same emotional wounds that came from being a child in a family living with alcoholism, and we both took on the role of protecting our mothers whilst our dads were out drinking. We could see in each other the roots of the pain and hurt we couldn't see in ourselves. The Big Guy's pain manifested in drinking too much while my pain manifested in loving too much. And our relationship brought out these demons in us both. The closer we became, the harder he felt his pain and the more he drank. The more he drank, the more I pushed to love him in a bid to save him from himself. At the time, I truly believed I had found my soulmate. I used to say he was the *other side of my coin.* And later on, I found out he was exactly that. He was the other side of my coin. He showed me the other side of mySelf, but it wasn't the bright shiny side I identified with, it was dark, tarnished and buried deep inside me. There were so many parallels in our lives and we felt very in tune with each other's experiences. Just as our father's paths had crossed when they were younger, so too had ours. The Big Guy actually remembered seeing me when I was younger. My first boyfriend lived in the same village where he grew up and one evening when we were out having dinner, The Big Guy turned to me and said, "*Dee, I saw you in a car with your boyfriend when you were younger. I filled his car up with petrol and looked in to see you sitting there staring out the window. I thought how beautiful you were. And I dreamed about you being my girlfriend.*"

He even had a tattoo of a young girl on his arm who looked just like me. This was his vision of a perfect woman. I became convinced she *was* me, and that the universe had finally brought us together. My ego went into overdrive and created a whole story about how we were long lost twin souls destined to be together, and how our union was divinely orchestrated to help us heal. In my fantasy world, I had us married and living in the country with dogs and horses in the fabulous house he had built. We even had a baby together. We travelled the world and had an amazing life. Of course, The Big Guy wasn't drinking or smoking in my fantasy, had lost weight and was eating healthily. And, of course, he was madly in love with me. It sounds laughably naïve, but I actually believed it all, even though the reality of our relationship was far from the princess fairytale I'd created in my head.

And then, three months in, the bubble burst and he said something that woke me up from my dream. We were having one of our famous Wednesday Wipeouts, where we'd meet with the intention of having a nice quiet dinner and a relaxing evening together, but end up drinking into the early hours of the morning and dancing round the living room to old '80s classics and Elvis songs, which he loved. I convinced myself it was OK. You always drink and party too much at the beginning of a new relationship, right? And he was like a big kid. He just wanted to play and escape his own dream, which in truth was a lot darker than mine. So there we were sipping wine at his house. He was telling me about the time he worked in television and how he 'lived the life', as he liked to call it. He got up to refill our glasses and as he headed towards the kitchen, he said, "*There's never a dull moment.*" I looked up at him and froze on the spot as those words pierced my soul. It was another red flag from the universe to wake me up. You see, until that day, I had only ever heard those words used by one other person: my dad. He would be propping up the bar, and as he finished one of his famous stories, he'd end the conversation with, "There's never a dull moment". You always knew you'd been entertained by Patsy Fallon when you heard those words – we even printed them on his funeral card. And here I was again faced with another significant message. It was the first of many opportunities I had to take a long, hard look at my relationship with The Big Guy and see it for what it really was, but of course at the time I didn't take it. I couldn't see that I was in a relationship with a man just like my dad, someone I loved but couldn't fix. I couldn't see that I'd tried to control my dad by being a good girl and I couldn't see that I was trying to control The Big Guy by showering him with love. I couldn't see that The Big Guy was lost to drink, just like my dad, and that he would never be there for me until he dealt with his issues – I had no right to try and change him. And I couldn't see that the universe was trying to teach me a lesson about me, not about The Big Guy or my dad. *Every* experience that comes to us is only ever given to teach us lessons about *ourselves,* not others. And this was a lesson about acceptance and control, a wakeup call for me to take responsibility for my actions and to 'own' the negative parts of me that I could see so easily in The Big Guy. The negative traits that I was quick to judge in him were also hiding out in the *part of me* I didn't want to see. There was a *part of me* in deep denial because I was so focused on the world outside myself and wasn't paying attention to the world inside me. But at the time I couldn't see. So I turned the lens on The Big Guy, blamed his drinking for pushing me away and exited the relationship. But it wasn't easy. This small, scratchy, niggling persistent voice *inside* kept saying, "*Who do you think you are, Dee? You're a single mum with two kids and three dead dads. Who will want you? You're lucky to have this man in your life.*"

And all I could hear was, "You're not worthy, you're not worthy, you're not worthy." My self-esteem was at rock bottom. I felt very damaged by my story, as if somehow I was a bad girl, as if it was my fault Martyn, Tony and Paul had died. The lack of compassion and love I showed my beautiful Self was shocking. And after just two weeks of being on my own I had a moment of weakness and let The Big Guy back in. And so we started another three-month merry go round of dating, where he went back to drinking too much and I went back to loving too much.

And that was how we rolled. Ours was a magnetic relationship of push/pull, attraction/repulsion, expansion/contraction, where two people muddled along two very different but intertwined paths. We fell into a cycle of broken promises, where I would leave after an explosive argument then return when he promised that things would get better. He talked a good game and promised everything, but never followed this up with action. Our whole relationship existed on his promise of achieving some unreachable goal in three months. He vowed to get fit and healthy, but it never happened. Then he asked me to give him three months to stop drinking. That definitely didn't happen. Then he needed the time to become financially secure. I bought into the promise and fixated on being with him to find my happiness, as he fixated on his own power, wealth and business to find his. He put all his effort and energy into building his business and working towards his plan for the future and left very little for me. But the more he pushed me away, the more I tried to hook into him to complete myself. He would constantly excuse his behaviour by saying, "I'm not there yet, Dee" and I would scream back, "But there is no there!". But in my own desperate need to be right, I missed how those words were meant for me as much as for him. You see, life only ever exists right here, right now, not in the future or the past. Every vital breath we take, every lesson we learn, unfolds naturally, just as it is supposed to. So whilst The Big Guy was waiting for his material success to manifest before he could find his peace, I was waiting on him to find mine. And if I'm truly honest with myself, I fell in love with the image of what this man promised. I fell in love with his potential, not the man who stood in front of me just as he was. I was so disconnected from my true feelings I failed to see I was desperately unhappy, and holding onto the dream wasn't helping me. But despite my unhappiness, something very profound happened when I met The Big Guy. Every time I saw something in him I didn't like, be it his drinking, his jealousy or his anger, it made me stop and look deep within myself and question my own behaviour. It was as if he reflected back a *part of me* I couldn't see. When I looked into his eyes it was as if the sadness and pain I saw were my own. I felt I was being drawn to him so I could observe my own suffering. The exchanges between us were so incredibly powerful, like a perfect balance of yin and yang energy, and at the time I didn't recognise myself when I was with him. It was like another person showed up, not sparkly Dee with her fairy dust, but an angry, needy, jealous woman, who I thought wasn't me at all, but, of course, she was. And so, after a year of struggling on in a relationship where I felt powerful yet weak, passionate yet destructive and experienced terrible pain yet great love, I finally found the courage to walk away for good. That was March 2015, or Magic March, as I liked to call it, because, as you'll find out later on in the book, it seemed that all roads lead to March.

I spent a year picking over my relationship with The Big Guy and trying to work out what it all meant. I racked my brains about what went wrong until finally my curiosity and need for answers brought me back to therapy again. By June 2016, my fabulous therapist had helped me put together the pieces and make sense of it all. When I told her my childhood story and the history of my romantic relationships, she could relate to what had been happening in my life, because she had been there herself. She understood what it was like to be *codependent*, which is the concept of losing oneself in the name of helping others, and is brilliantly explained in the book *Codependent No More – How to Stop Controlling Others and Start Caring for Yourself* by Melody Beattie. The author describes how people develop their individual self or *emotional identity* as an extension of the family experience throughout their childhood and into adulthood. If the family view was one where the child was encouraged to be seen and not heard and prevented from expressing their feelings openly, or if their so-called good feelings were rewarded while their bad feelings were punished, then the child becomes *Enmeshed*. Enmeshed children have a false sense of self and develop an outer persona that is at odds with their true self. They can feel everyone else's feelings, but not their own. They learn to hold on, shut down and dissociate from their feelings and they fixate on others. This is what codependency is, and it leads to disappointment and feelings of rejection in relationships where a person constantly compromises their needs to feed the desires of another. They become afraid to speak their truth because this might lead to more abandonment, which is the demon to the codependent. And this was me all over. Learning about codependency has probably been the single most valuable lesson in my life. It has helped me to finally take responsibility for my story, and to take responsibility for my experience with The Big Guy. My issues with codependency were just as damaging as his issues with alcohol. A codependent is a woman who loves too much, and in the book of the same title, by Robin Norwood [13] explains that denial and control are the two key characteristics of this type of woman.

> *"The practice of denial, magnanimously rephrased as 'overlooking his faults' or 'keeping a positive attitude,' conveniently sidesteps the two-to-tango aspect of how his*

shortcomings allow her to practice her familiar roles. When her drive to control masquerades as 'being helpful' and 'giving encouragement' what is ignored again is her own need for superiority and power implied in this kind of interaction."

And that's just the thing with codependency, it is very easy to hide behind the person who is the alcoholic, and blame them for what's going wrong in our life. Excessive drinking gave me a viable excuse to say, "Look what you did to me," but in truth nobody ever does anything to me. I bring on my own suffering. Let's face it, very few people would choose to be in a relationship with an alcoholic. By the nature of their disease, alcoholics are inherently selfish, regularly lie to cover up their deceit and are financially irresponsible. They're not the ideal candidates for a perfect match. You would have thought someone like me, who grew up in a family with alcoholism, would have known better. But the patterns we develop in childhood are deeply entrenched into our psyche and often take years to reveal themselves, as was my experience. My lessons have not come easily to me. I have held on to a lot of denial and stubbornness, and I'm still learning to make peace with myself. Acceptance has been the key to my freedom.

"Acceptance is the antithesis of denial and control. It is a willingness to recognise what reality is and to allow that reality to be, without a need to change it. Therein lies a

happiness that issues not from manipulating outside conditions or people, but from developing inner peace, even in the face of challenges and difficulties" [14]

And as I started to make peace with myself, my second biggest discovery was learning about the Shadow Self, *the part of me* I couldn't see.

According to Carl Jung[15], the conscious and unconscious mind are organised into different 'selves' or archetypes. Archetypes are models of people, behaviours and personalities that live within us.

The Ego is the most identifiable as it resides in our conscious awareness and is essentially how we relate to the external world through our feelings, thinking and intuition. Jung believed that consciousness is selective and The Ego chooses the most relevant information from the environment, depending on how we've been programmed and conditioned as a child. The rest of the information sinks into the unconscious mind. This may then appear later in the form of dreams or visions.

The Persona is the 'veil'. It is the self that we would like the world to see, and it changes depending on who we're with. It's the side of the self that we show at work, home or at play. So I can be a mother, or yogi, or a sex goddess (I wish!). The Persona is often made up of all the positive characteristics that we identify with and want to show to others, such as kindness, love, generosity, compassion, etc., and if we are akin to people pleasing, The Persona will grow exponentially, but so too will the Shadow Self, which is the 'twin'.

The Shadow is the other side of the coin. It contains all the traits we dislike and don't want to see in ourselves, such as greed, jealousy, anger and fear.

To achieve wholeness as a human being, we need to perceive our experiences in life through a process of opposites. This is because life, in its essence, is made up of opposing forces. Left vs right, good vs bad, light vs dark, yin vs yang. One cannot exist without the other, and vice versa. So, to experience the fullness of life we need to integrate the Persona and the Shadow into our conscious mind. This means being able to accept and explore the shadow side of ourselves. In doing so we create spiritual balance, healing and wholeness. If we deny the Shadow Self, if we do not claim and use it, it will project itself onto others. This means we draw into our lives people who have the qualities *we cannot stand*, as we fail to see that we have them in ourselves. And this is exactly what happened in my experience with The Big Guy.

The part of me I now know of as *the Shadow* took centre stage in our relationship. As I became repulsed by The Big Guy's drinking, arrogance and jealousy, something inside me clicked. I exploded into tyrannical rants of anger and jealousy that seemed to consume me and were totally out of character. I regularly stormed out of restaurants, I criticised and judged and I was bloody vicious in my opinion, to the point where

I sounded like some evangelical preacher. When I was with The Big Guy, I often felt like a crazed woman who was out of control and didn't know her mind. Being with him seemed to stir up so much venom and anger inside, and I would sit for hours crying as I tried to make sense of what was happening to me. This extreme reaction came around because I lived behind a façade of denial and was trying to control life.

"When a person is living behind a front, a façade, his unexpressed feelings pile up to some explosion point, and are then apt to be triggered by some specific incident... The angry flare-up over one annoyance in the relationship may actually be the pent-up or denied feelings resulting from dozens of such situations. But in the context in which it is expressed it is unreasonable and hence not understood." [16]

My personality was completely polarised. I lived on the edges and only saw the world in terms of black and white. I was stuck in my childhood ways of compartmentalising life into good and bad experiences, and the Shadow was trying to help me integrate these opposite ways of being to bring me back to the middle ground, which is balanced and whole. Repression of the Shadow Self and our negative emotions is one of the main barriers to self-love. And this ultimately is what life taught me through my relationship with The Big Guy. Like me, he was living in a place of darkness and depression caused by his childhood pain. But now I could see my Shadow and she was guiding me out of the darkness towards the light. We can work with the Shadow in many ways, and one of the best is via creative activities, such as writing, painting, dancing or making music. This is because creation cannot happen without the fusing of opposites. Creation is the fusion of male and female, which in itself is the antithesis of our Shadow. When I started writing a daily journal I allowed myself the space to download all the stuff I had been holding onto in my Shadow. I allowed myself to spew out all my anger, frustration and bitterness as I ranted onto the page. And it felt good. I also created characters for my Shadow and Persona, and I invited them to play in my stories. My Persona is hippy Dee. She has long, brown flowing locks, a soft cherub face and she wears a floaty white lace dress and a daisy chain in her hair. She smiles sunshine, is fresh faced and full of joy. Delilah is the other side. She's a kickass peroxide blonde with a short pixie crop. She wears black latex hot pants and a face full of angst. You do not want to mess with Delilah! And as I started imagining my characters; what their lives were like, where they lived and who they dated, etc., I started to find pieces of my shattered life, aspects of myself that had been lost in the wilderness through years of repression.

"What's the greatest lesson a woman should learn?
that since day one, she's already had everything

she needs within herself, it's the world
that convinced her she did not."

Rupi Kaur

And I learnt that the Shadow isn't just one person. There are many facets that make up who we are, and these archetypal energies that make us a man or a woman all have their own Shadow side. And this journey into the shadow is taking me on one hell of a ride. It's taking me into my womb, the womb of the creatrix, and into the goddess. The process of unravelling the Shadow will, I suspect, be a lifelong quest, since it has taken me many lifetimes to accumulate all the pain and suffering that I carry with me today. And that's OK – I accept it. But for now, I am grateful that I am able to release my control on life and accept the parts of me I have denied for years. I'm being gentle as I walk this path, and bit by bit I'm allowing myself to release the anger, jealousy and sadness that I put into the 'bad' box as a child. I am becoming more comfortable with dealing with these feelings and I'm no longer nervous about expressing them in public. I speak my mind more often, and I'm no longer passive aggressive. If I'm angry, I'm not afraid to show it. And what's most interesting, as my therapist explained, is that as I'm owning these 'negative' feelings, I seem to be attracting less negative experiences into my world. So, for example, I am getting into fewer angry confrontations with my teenage daughter, and I'm dealing with my inner pain and sadness to the point that everyday life feels so much more enjoyable.

And as for my relationship with The Big Guy, well, we danced the dance of codependency on and off since we split in March 2015. It took me a further year to wean myself off and cut the deep chords of attachment I had to him. We met as friends on many occasions, but I felt uncomfortable in his presence because it felt like I was feeding an addiction, and I could sense this pull to want to fix him. As I gradually learnt to distance and protect myself, I had to stand my ground and claim my space. And even though there will always be *part of me* that will be truly grateful for the lessons he brought, for now, I have put him back in the shadows where he came from.

9

Bargaining With MySelf

"How people treat you is their Karma, how you react is yours."

Wayne Dyer

As those first three months drew to a close, I can honestly say I have never felt so utterly raw or vulnerable. My whole way of being had been called into question via my relationships with others and my childhood experiences. Life was teaching me so much. As the veil started to lift and I opened to the world around me, and as I became more in tune with my body, I felt more connected to the source of life that is drawn from Mother Earth and travels through the chakra system to nourish and feed the soul. This energy passes into the first chakra, Muladhara, where the foundation of our being is created, up to the second chakra, Svadhisthana, where we seek freedom through movement and let go of attachment to the mother/child bond. The second chakra is about finding peace in opposites, as we learn about separation when we crawl or walk for the first time and discover the wonders of the world on our own. We leave our mother's side and embrace the world of our own unique selves. As adults, we learn to cut the umbilical cord to others 'out there', and realise the only thing that matters is the world we create inside ourselves. The second chakra is where we develop our emotional identity and learn to receive and express the full spectrum of emotions in a healthy and balanced way. And we get in touch with these emotions through the act of movement.

> *"Movement is the song of the body. Yes, the body has its own song from which the movement of dancing arises spontaneously. This song, if you can listen to it, is beauty."* [17]

As the body moves, it responds to the vibration of the 'song' by contracting and expanding. When we are fearful, the body contracts and becomes small, the muscles tighten and we feel stress in our tissues. Contraction of the body usually indicates that a person is stuck in some area of their life. When this happens, the body will feel heavy and exhausted and these trapped feelings will eventually express themselves through ill health. On the other hand, when we are at peace, the body feels expansive. There is an openness and lightness in every cell. Freedom comes from this fluidity. As the life force extends beyond its form, the body feels physically bigger than its human shell. Expansion allows us to access the infinite wisdom of the unconscious mind, where pure love resides. Through expansion, one transcends time and matter to join forces with the collective power of the universe from the deep well of truth that all humanity has access to. These moments of expansion come when we are truly connected both to ourselves and the world around us.

It feels euphoric to experience such moments, and in late spring 2015, I had my first glimpse of what it truly meant to be connected. I had just finished a month's sobriety, where for the first time in my life, other than when I was pregnant or nursing my babies, I stepped off the social treadmill that consumed my life and gave myself 30 alcohol-free days to clear my body and mind. I knew it was something I needed to do. I knew that sobriety would help me open up to the feelings that had long become stagnant in my body and were aching to find a way out. And, as I sat in silence with my thoughts each day, I could feel a little piece of me reveal itself. All I needed to do was sit in silence, observe my thoughts and let whatever was trapped in my body come to the surface. When the feelings opened to the silence there was a moment of acknowledgement – then they were gone. Years of holding on, of denial, of fear passed before me in those moments of silence. It was the start of letting go, and the start of understanding the second chakra. Letting go, as I have said before, is not easy for me, but this was 'the work' I needed to do to cut my codependent behaviour.

However, those two little words have held on tight and showed themselves as deeply stubborn and resistant. As I started to release and unravel part of my being, I found myself drawn deeper into another level of self that needed healing. This cycle of observing, revealing and releasing is how I worked through much of my past and healed the wounds of the heart, to find my peace for now. And finding my peace is an ongoing process. As I evolve and change as a person, I'm faced with new challenges that require a fresh level of balance and understanding as I go deeper into myself.

I talk about wanting to find peace rather than happiness, because I believe happiness is a temporary emotion. Happiness has a counterbalance in sadness, and both emotions need a place to breathe if one is to live a balanced, wholesome life. When we live from a place that's only focused on happiness we're being one-dimensional. We live a half-life that misses the fullness of reality. On the other hand, when we live a life that searches out peace, we allow ourselves to accept what is. Peace makes space for the darker times in life, as well as the brighter ones. But how do we find peace in our everyday lives? According to the renowned humanitarian H.H Pujya Swami Chidanand Saraswatiji, we can achieve it by doing three things. First, we must allow meditation to become our lives. We should begin slowly by *meditating* for a few minutes in the morning and evening, focusing on the oneness of all beings and connecting with the divine. Eventually, through years of practice, our whole life becomes a moving meditation and we can become one with life. The second thing we must do is learn to be calm in our lives, and to not *react* to things that happen around us. We become like the ocean, the waves coming and going and being gentle or wild, but the ocean remaining ever present and contained. So many times our mood changes as a reaction to other people's behavior, but when we are at peace we don't allow others to switch us on and off like that. We simply have no reaction to the waves in life and do not give power to others in this way. Spiritual practice helps us achieve the inner strength needed to remain calm in all situations. It helps us meet life with waves of silence.

Finally, we learn *introspection*. We learn to sit with ourselves at night and review our actions with compassion, knowing that we have within ourselves the grace to change at any moment to be the best we can in this world.

So, as spring drew to a close and I embraced the process of letting go, I became increasingly aware that my outer world was a true reflection of my inner feelings. And the way to bring peace and harmony to my experiences in the world outside was to bring peace and harmony to my inner world. We are all ultimately responsible for creating our reality, and this reality is a mirror of what we truly feel inside. The people and experiences we draw into our lives come to us to teach us lessons so that our souls can evolve in consciousness to a higher realm. The way we experience life is, of course, influenced by our family and our environment, so by nature and nurture, but also by our karma. Karma is the law of cause and effect, or, to quote from the Bible, "You reap what you sow."

Most people are born with a karmic debt of some sort, and when we experience difficulties in life that seem unexplainable, it's usually because we are paying off a debt from a previous life. We work with karma in this life in the hope we'll pass on to the next one as more evolved human beings – or not! Kindness and compassion reaps rewards in this life and the next, whereas negative acts bring pain and suffering. There is no escaping ourselves, because if we have been truly dreadful in this life, the law of karma means it will manifest in some way in the next one.

Through karma we have the means to understand the suffering and inequality in the world. I have often questioned how my children were born into a world of comparative wealth when others are born into a world of poverty. How can one man live to be a 100 when another lives for just one day? How can one person suffer deep depression when another lives in relative peace? People who come into this life and suffer terrible strife do so because they've carried this temperament from a past life. That doesn't mean to say that if you are born poor this is how life will be. There is always an opportunity to turn suffering into bliss, just as the reverse is true. Someone born into great privilege can lead a life filled with suffering because of the choices they make. On an individual soul level, we are all uniquely different, but collectively each person on earth contributes towards the consciousness of humanity, which *in itself* is whole and complete. So the rich balance out the poor, kind people balance out the unkind, the old balance out the young, and so on. It is this collective consciousness, this oneness of life, which binds us together. And we can raise our consciousness, and the collective consciousness of the world, by healing our karma. As we evolve as beings we learn to recognise the patterns and behaviours in our life through the signs and symbols we receive from the universe. We can choose to travel our path with ease and accept the signs and lessons along the way, even if at times those lessons bring pain and suffering. Or we can choose to exert our own free will and live with the consequences of whatever those decisions might bring us.

"Synchronicity is the Universe saying, "You're getting warmer"

Michelle Risi

When I talk about 'being' in the flow, I'm referring to being on this path and accepting whatever each day brings with an open heart and the freedom to receive, observe and react to it. So, what are the 'signs' the universe gives us to show that we are on the right path? Well, the most notable ones are: experiencing synchronistic events, seeing number sequences, hearing a poignant piece of music, seeing feathers, connecting to nature and observing spirit animals.

Carl Jung believed events may be connected by meaning.[18] Synchronistic events happen all the time, and they tend to stop us in our tracks as we realise the significance of the meaning behind them. Jung discovered there was no logical explanation for these 'meaningful coincidences' other than they had special meaning for the person experiencing them.

The power of synchronicity has revealed itself many times in my life, but most poignantly the night before Tony died, when I sent him a text telling him I wasn't ready to lose him. That message haunted me in the early days after he died, and I questioned how I could possibly have known what was about to happen to him. There was, of course, no way of knowing, but somehow those words still came from me. They were the last exchange I had with the man I loved, and I truly believe they came from a higher place to protect me from the suffering of his loss. I believe those words came from a moment in time when the boundary between my inner and outer reality dissolved and the universe opened to reveal itself. My husband's path was his to walk alone, and I believe he was always destined to die on 26th June 2010 on Ben Nevis. That was his path, and he crossed my path to show me what it meant to be loved. Tony loved me completely and accepted me for who I was, but now it was up to me to give that same love to myself.

Ever since Tony's death, the universe has knocked itself out to send me signs my inner world is aligned with my outer reality. Another mind-blowing example of synchronicity happened when I took the children on holiday to Thailand in July 2015. We were taking an overnight flight so the children went to school in the morning as usual, and I planned to finish off a few last-minute chores. I dropped Fionn at school and headed into town. As I approached the main roundabout into the city centre the front tyre blew on my car. Somehow this wasn't unexpected. I'd sensed something was about to happen as I approached the busy roundabout at rush hour. I remember thinking, "Oh, God, please just get me round safely."

As I crawled round to the sound of blaring horns from drivers impatiently scurrying to work in the rush hour madness, I willed my car out of trouble and onto a nearby slip road. The front left wheel tyre was completely flat, all the air had gone and the wheel hung off the car. I was going nowhere. As I got out of the car and looked down at the lifeless tyre, I realised I was quite literally stuck. I sat on the grass verge with my head in my hands and heaviness in my heart. I knew the lifeless wheel was a reflection of my life. It was a profound shout out from the universe for me to take a long hard look at my life and make a change. At the time I was struggling to let go of The Big Guy and still held on to the dream that I might somehow miraculously fix him and have my happy ever after. I was still obsessively attached to him, even though we'd split in March, and my friendship with him was hurting me by feeding my codependency. In my moment of vulnerability, I called him and he came to my rescue to sort out my car.

By doing so, I let him back into my heart again, and another five months of torment followed as I struggled to let go of the relationship and move on with my life.

Then, five months later on 18th December 2015, I had an epiphany. It was on the day I flew to India with my children for Christmas. I was having lunch with my friend Taran, and when I left to pick up Fionn I noticed that the front tyre on the left-hand side of the car was completely flat. I mean, what are the chances of that happening again? I looked at Taran in complete amazement and told her about what had happened to me in July, and how I'd allowed myself to get sucked back into the hopeless drama with The Big Guy. But this time things were different.

"Dee, you don't need a man to sort this out," Taran said. "We have each other and the AA!"

And with those words, Taran sprung into action and helped me. I no longer felt vulnerable and stuck. In that moment I broke the chains of codependency and finally found the strength to leave The Big Guy in the shadows once and for all. It was the catalyst for complete change. From that point on, my life took a totally unexpected turn. It brought me to India, and from there the magic really happened.

The next sign came in the form of numbers. When I started seeing recurring number sequences, I knew it was a nudge the universe was trying to communicate with me. The most common number sequence that people tend to see when they have a spiritual awakening is 11:11. This carries the vibration of new beginnings and is a message to listen to the divine wisdom within. Throughout May 2015, I could barely go anywhere without seeing 11:11. I would randomly look up from what I was doing and there it was on my digital clock in my car, or on my phone, or on the timer of my cooker or a billboard at the side of the road. There just seemed to be no hiding from 11:11. Seeing it reminded me to stop and reflect on whatever it was that was consuming me and to really listen to the silent voice inside for guidance. Seeing numbers all around me made me feel protected. As I learnt to decipher their meaning, I opened up to a new conversation with the universe. At the time I was reading a book called *Zero Limits* by Joe Vitale and Ihaleakala Hew Len. It's based on the ancient Hawaiian teachings of Ho'oponopono[19], which is the practice of mental cleansing and forgiveness. It came to me at a perfect time when I needed to 'own' my inner world and accept responsibility for some of the more unpleasant things that were happening in my life. This book blew my mind. The philosophy and teaching of Ho'oponopono is so beautifully simple that it had a profound effect on the way I interacted with the world around me.

The book tells the story of one of the authors, Ihaleakala Hew Len, a Hawaiian psychologist who healed a mental hospital full of criminally insane patients without ever meeting a single one of them. He examined their case files before turning the lens on himself. The essential edict of this healing modality is that we are all 100% responsible for ourselves. This means every experience we see, feel, hear, touch and taste is a projection of our inner reality. And if we are 100% responsible for the experiences that come into our presence, we are 100% responsible for resolving them. In order to resolve the actions of the world, we need to go deep inside our own selves and clean out the negative thoughts and ideas until nothing is left. And when nothing is left, the space is filled with love and we go back to our divinely created self. That love is then transmuted to every situation we enter into.

Like I said, it is mind-blowing stuff and it struck a chord with me at a time when I was ready to listen. For me, being open to Ho'oponopono was the ultimate answer to my codependency. Put simply, after a lifetime of fixating on others, here I was being shown that my first and only job was to fixate on myself. And the way to do this is via the mantra,

"I love you. I'm sorry. Please forgive me. Thank you."

Repeating this mantra over and over again helps to clean memories from the subconscious mind until it returns to the zero state of creation, which is limitless and boundless. I was going to finish this section by encouraging you all to read this amazing book, but then I realised I would be missing the point. Instead, I reminded myself that maybe it was time for *me* to read it again.

"The purpose of life is to be restored back to love, moment to moment. To fulfil this purpose, the individual must acknowledge that he is 100% responsible for creating his life the way it is. He must come to see that it is his thoughts that create his life the way it is moment to moment. The problem is not people, places and situations, but rather the thoughts of them. He must come to appreciate there is no such thing as 'out there'"

– Dr Ihaleakala Hew Len.

Music was my next big spiritual discovery. I have always loved and listened to music, but it wasn't until late spring that I began to feel as if I was being sent messages through song lyrics. Music is a universal language that transcends culture and religion. I truly believe that it has the power to unite us all. Whenever I needed reassurance and guidance, I'd turn the radio on and a song would play that spoke to my soul. Every time. Without fail.

"Music is a moral law. It gives souls to the universe, wings to the mind, flight to the imagination, and charm and gaiety to life, and to everything."

Plato

As music became the soundtrack to my awareness, finding feathers became the visual indicator of the angelic love that is there for us all, if we can just open our hearts and minds to see it. Finding little white feathers was my greatest comfort in the long, lonely days after Tony died. They helped me explain the concept of life after death to my son Fionn and to Tony's nieces and nephews, as they struggled with their own grief. I remember playing with the children at Tony's mother's house not long after he died. I told them stories about how he used to pick them up and throw them around until they screamed with delight. The children smiled as they remembered the fun times they had with their beloved Tony, but their smiles were also tinged with sadness because they felt his loss terribly. As I held their sadness in my heart, I realised I needed a way to explain to them that Tony was always there with them. I looked down amongst the Lego and saw a little white feather sitting there. I picked it up and said, "Look, it's a feather from Tony, he's letting you know that he's here with you."

And from that day on, every time the children saw a little white feather they put it in their pockets to remind them of their special Tony. In those raw early days of my bereavement, those little white feathers showed up everywhere. And although my heart was heavy with grief, I knew it was Tony whispering to me, "It's OK, Dee, I'm here, my love."

The feathers helped me see a world beyond physical death as I let in the angels, and asked them for help and guidance. I always knew the angelic realm was there, but I kind of didn't want to believe in it. But my pain was too great to ride it alone and I needed help. So I prayed to God and asked for signs from the angels to help me. I studied a mountain of literature on angel therapy and connected online with oracle readings, which resonated with me on such a deep level that I felt they were talking to me personally. And in some ways they were, through the collective consciousness of the higher vibrational angels. I battled with my senses, often questioning what I was doing and wondering if I was going completely mad, but somehow there was a calmness that brought me back. I felt myself shifting from my old way of doing, of controlling or pulling for things to happen, to this new place, a place that was rooted in spirituality and esoteric thinking. Initially it felt uncomfortable, or, if I'm honest, just plain weird, as my thinking mind fought hard to protect the ego, but my feeling heart wanted to feed my soul with love. But I always came back to my prayers, back to the angels and my daily visualisation and affirmations. I eventually won the battle between heart and mind and accepted that I am blessed to receive angelic guidance. I am a spirit from the angelic realm living here on earth. This IS who I am. This is me. I didn't choose it, and I sure as hell have fought against it, but there is no denying that this IS me. I no longer need to hide.

"With all my cells
relishing the waters of life
from formless hands if light
ecstasy flows through
to unlock the treasure chest inside"

Narayan

Feathers have different meanings according to their colour. When I started to receive Reiki healing, I first noticed black and grey ones. Reiki is a form of hands-on healing where spiritually guided universal energy is transferred from practitioner to client. I must admit, I was slightly sceptical about its effectiveness until I had a treatment with an amazing girl called Jodi. She literally made me vibrate when she laid her hands on me. The sensation was so intense it was like I was plugged into a power station – I was sold. I started having regular monthly Reiki treatments and after a particularly powerful session in early June 2015, where I felt a major release and shift in my energy, I returned home to find a big pile of black feathers on my front lawn. I couldn't quite believe what I was seeing so I ran inside and Googled the meaning (what would we do without Google, hey?). Black feathers signify a healing has taken place, and there was no denying that it had. The Reiki had worked its magic by cleaning my energy and leaving me with this feeling of intense love in my heart.

The final sign that showed me I was awakening to my inner self was an increased sensitivity to the natural world around me, and to the animal world.

"It is our natural condition to be at one with the earth and universe. The sages of old understood this. When our microcosm, the energies we hold at a cellular level, matches the macrocosm, the world outside our body, there is nothing that we cannot do. We were born to dream and then through our expanding consciousness to make those dreams reality."

As I grew in awareness, my antennae to the magic of the world around me became more finely tuned. And when this happened the universe started to reveal itself through the wonder of nature and from the animals we share this beautiful planet with. To be at one with nature is to align the inner world with the outer world, and when this happens we open to infinite possibilities. We become sensitive to our environment, our bodies crave fresh, seasonal food and our habits and behaviours align with the four seasons. As the soul moves to the rhythm and grace of the seasons, we move through the full emotional spectrum of human experience. In spring, we awaken to the possibilities of new beginnings as we plant the seeds for new projects and watch the earth spring to life from its wintery slumber. Summer is a time to party as the days are warmer and longer, and the spirit is freer and lighter. In the autumn, we take stock in preparation for the long winter months and show gratitude for the abundance of summer. As the leaves fall from the trees, we take time to release and let go. In winter, we hibernate and rest, just as the animals do. It is a time to quieten the mind, still the soul and reflect on life. As I moved through the seasons, I found myself beginning to deeply appreciate the colour and texture of the landscape around me, from the barren frosty days of winter through to the lush vibrant growth of spring, the dry dusty haze of summer and the warm mood of autumn. And, as the light in me grew ever stronger, my vision of the world around me intensified. I started to notice so much more detail and vibrancy. The sky became alive and talked to me through the clouds. The woods at the back of my house where I walked my dog, Yogi, seemed to feed me with ideas for my writing, and the butterflies and pigeons became my constant companions. I could feel this magic when I was out in nature, and somehow I knew Mother Earth was healing me. I knew it was all connected.

The woods breathed so much life and pleasure into my soul and it was where this book came into being; my ideas were born out of every footstep. I used to receive the wood's wisdom and write notes on my phone. I sensed something magical was happening. Then one day, when I took Yogi for her daily exercise, I saw a bulldozer rip the heart out of that magical place. I was floored. I felt the tears of the trees as my heart broke and I welled up. I couldn't bear to see this mindless destruction, and for what? Money? To build more concrete houses? As I watched them cut down those beautiful trees it was as if they were stealing the ground from underneath me too. My beautiful, magical woods, which had given so much life, were being robbed of their own. My inner world was truly feeling the pain of my outer world, and it was telling me I too was in pain. I could feel the separation from Mother Earth and knew it was a sign to go deeper and reconcile my own suffering.

This is when I turned to the second chakra, called Svadhisthana in Sanskrit. This means sweetness. And sweetness was something I was all too familiar with, as it was my default nature in relationships. My past boyfriends often described me as being sweet, much to my utter disapproval. I mean, what self-respecting woman wants to be called sweet? I wanted to be seen as cool or quirky or amazing, I did not want to be seen as bloody sweet. But of course, what others could see in me was more often than not a truer reflection than what I could see in myself. At the time, like it or not, I was overly sweet, especially in my romantic relationships. I was full on sweetness and light and bent over backwards to please, putting my partners' needs before mine like the perfect Stepford wife. And this sweetness showed itself in my body in my excessive second chakra, which is located around the region of the lower back, abdomen, hips and genitals. My hips naturally sway forward in their enthusiasm to please others, and this for me was the clue to everything, the piece of the jigsaw that I had been missing for all those years. You see, the second chakra is primarily concerned with a person's emotional identity and sexuality. People with excessive second chakras are needy and fixate on others as a way of compensating for their own lack of emotional attention as a child. They are overly giving and seek attachment to others to feed themselves energetically. They are the classic codependents that I talked about in the previous chapter. Their bodies are either small or large and are always very soft, almost sponge-like. They are often hypermobile in their joints. But they are overly emotional and suffer from poor boundaries because the first and third chakras are deficient. This means they are unable to contain their emotions, which end up spilling out into other areas of their life. And this was me. Even though I struggled with this notion of neediness, there was no escaping from the truth. I needed to bring my second chakra into balance, and to do this I had to learn to contain my emotions by strengthening my root so that I could learn to trust myself again. I did this through the work of the first chakra, where I healed my childhood pain. Understanding the chakras and how they related to my psychological development was like opening a doorway to a deeper appreciation of my body. I developed a new level of understanding through my yoga practice as I started to fully appreciate the sheer power of the ancient magical healing system. It took me six years to finetune the song of my body, which had been faithful to me all along.

My body finally showed me how my weakness in my Mulahadara (root/first chakra) was related to my childhood story and my pent-up sadness that was crying out to be released. This sadness had been locked away for years and had finally found its way to the surface. Now, every time I step on my mat, I know that when I ground my feet I'm building a strong base to grow and heal as a person. My body also showed me that my core needed to be strengthened. There was a disconnect between my root and my core, and no matter how hard I tried to engage it in difficult postures, I just seemed to fall over. Then I would give up.

Incidentally, the will is related to the third chakra, Manipura, and a person's wants and desires. I had a profound sense that I was starting to address this as I began to question what it was I wanted in life. And the truth was I just didn't know. I was at a crossroads. I was fighting against the traditions and culture of my past, and everything that life brought me, and I desired to be free and no longer bound by conformity. Everything I believed I wanted, such as marriage, money, status and a great job, had come to me, but there I was in 2015 unsure of it all. I didn't know what I wanted anymore and I felt very compromised. This conflict between heart and mind, ego and self, the duality of opposing ideas was very much the heartland for second chakra healing. This comes from the integration of mind and body, but also from how we bargain with our inner and outer reality. This bargaining happens when the soul awakens and starts to find meaning from experiences in the material realm.

Summer 2015

The summer of 2015 was about freedom and growth as I searched for self-love, acceptance and my identity. I began to observe life with a fresh pair of eyes, which were now turned on me, as I questioned what it was I wanted. As I stood staring at myself in front of the mirror one morning, I looked myself square in the eyes and asked: "What do you want, Dee?" There was no answer. The blankness filled the air as I searched for a clue. All I knew was that I no longer wanted what I had. I sensed that I needed to step out of the mould of conventional living, which was bound by materialism, labouring from nine to five to feed the pockets of big corporations and following a system that is fuelled by capitalism and conformity. I needed to create something more meaningful *for me*. I sensed this deeply, but I didn't know what lay on the other side. I had to take a leap of faith in the knowledge that whatever was there was better than what I had now. It meant closing the door on my old life, which at times was scary. Over the summer, as I watched my cousin get married in the same church I'd tied the knot in 11 years earlier in 2004, I grieved for everything that I'd lost. I was still very attached to the idea of marriage and the little girl's dream, and I suffered greatly as I fought with the desire to merge with another. The summer of 2015 taught me about the roots of suffering, and the second noble truth of Buddhism, which is that suffering arises from attachment to desires. My need to hold on was hurting me deeply. I was fearful of the blank canvas that lay before me if I closed the door, and I needed to strengthen my will and open my heart by healing the third and fourth chakras. The third chakra is concerned with the process of individuation, which is a willingness to step out of the familiar and expected and confront the challenge of uncertainty.[20] Meanwhile, the fourth chakra is concerned with self-love, healing the wounded heart from grief, and integrating the inner female and male archetypes, which Jung called the anima and animus. [21]

Summer was also about having fun and enjoying the long hazy days of lightness, where the heart opens to all possibilities. There is no shadow and no place to hide from the self as we step out bravely and grow courageously. In summer, we are warmed by the fire of the sun and the fierce determination of the soul. The summer of 2015 blessed me with the following important lessons:

- ***We need to know what we want in order to manifest it.*** Sounds obvious, I know, but if we don't know where we are headed we will never know how to get there. Having a clear understanding of what it is we want from life requires will, determination and belief. Everything is possible if we take a leap of faith and don't give in.
- ***We need to let go of attachment to outcome.*** When we know what we want, we need to trust it will come to us through the right action. If we hold on to our desires, we bring fear energy into play and more often than not move further away from our outcome rather than closer to it.
- ***We need an open heart to receive love.*** A closed heart can take nothing in and feels empty. It's a lonely place to be. The only way to open the heart is to love the self. Loving the self really is the only work that matters.
- ***We need to find our inner goddess.*** The masculine energies of the world have prevailed for so long that the female energy feels hidden. It's time to liberate our inner goddess and bring this soft and nurturing love to heal ourselves and our world.

10

Letting Go Of Anger

"'No'

might make them angry.

but

it will make you free

– if no one has ever told you, your freedom is

more important than their anger."[22]

Anger is the ugly side of grief. And I was mostly unaware of my own anger until it surfaced, often in an unexpected rage, leaving me utterly shocked, as I questioned where the hell it had come from. I had so much anger in me and it held itself in my tight shoulders and through my need for control. It left me shaken, raw and vulnerable and my outbursts were mostly misdirected at my children and family. Releasing anger is about reclaiming our right to object to the things that hurt us. It's about being able to stand confident in our power in the knowledge that we will not be punished for objecting to something. It's about the power to say no. Over time, I started to release bit by bit, as I gave myself permission to feel anger and addressed the pains of the past I had held on to so tightly. As I strengthened my fire and will, I had the energy to release and the freedom to say 'no' to pleasing others and 'yes' to pleasing me. And there was no hiding the fire of truth during the summer of 2015, as life showed me the value of letting go and I finally stood my ground and questioned what it was I wanted.

I spent the first three weeks of the summer in Asia, visiting Thailand with the children, seeing the sights of Bangkok and the amazing Golden Palace, and chilling out on the beautiful island of Koh Samui and soaking up the white sands and warm sea air. I loved being in the East and felt more connected to myself there than I did in the Western world. Something inside seemed to come alive when I was on Asian soil and I genuinely found a peace that didn't exist at home. And that trip to Thailand in July 2015 somehow planted a seed of possibility for another way of being. As I left Asia with a heavy heart, I felt a longing to return as soon as possible.

The day after my return, I had to make a very different trip. This time it was to Ireland for my cousin Helen's wedding. Helen is the youngest daughter of my Aunt Betty – my mother's sister. She married Ciaron on 1st August 2015 in

Tipperary Town, which is where my family is from in Ireland. They married in St Michael's Church, where Tony and I had become husband and wife 11 years earlier. I knew this was an opportunity to close the door on my marriage and my old life and finally let go. I knew it was going to be difficult to step back into that church and watch Helen and Ciaran pledge their love for each other in front of God, just as Tony and I had done 11 years earlier, but it was something I had to do. I'd only been back to that church once, which was to visit the priest for a blessing a few months after Tony's death. I remember feeling so saddened by God's great betrayal and by the senseless loss and the feeling of injustice that Tony's death had brought. It wasn't just the injustice for him, it was mine too – how could God rob me of my dream, my identity, my future, my life , my everything? After all, I was a good person. I suppose I must have been very angry at the time, but I didn't allow this anger to surface. Instead, it lay dormant in me for years and bubbled away inside. Now my anger was ready to explode. I knew the wedding would open old wounds of longing for the life I once had, but somehow I knew it was time to move through the pain and release it.

"How lucky I am to have something that
makes saying goodbye so hard."

A.A.Milne

Irish weddings are big events and go on for days. Well, at least they do in my family. Day one is the initial gathering where everyone meets again and catches up on life. Day two is the main event – the wedding itself – where the female guests pull out all the stops on the glamour stakes, and there's usually a competition for who has the best outfit and the biggest hat. And day three is the after party for those who still have the stamina, where the bride and groom get to really let their hair down. Quite frankly, I was dreading it all and reluctant about going. I wanted to see my beautiful cousin Helen get married and catch up with my extended family because, as families go, we are very close. We all get along really well and we really like each other, which is amazing considering there are about 80 of us. There have been no major fallouts or old rifts hidden in our history – at least not to my knowledge! But I was also anxious about the drinking. You see, I knew I wouldn't be able to tolerate the effects of alcohol on my clean yoga body. Alcohol these days just seems to leave me feeling very low and negative, as if it has some sort of toxic emotional quality to it. If I drink too much a dark mood descends on me and I feel so depressed for days; I figure it's just not worth it. But despite all the physical and emotional effects that alcohol had on my body, back then I didn't always know my limits, and so whenever I was due to attend a big social event I usually spent a few days beforehand slightly dreading the thought of it, which in hindsight is actually quite sad.

And so I travelled to Ireland on Friday 31st July under the powerful energetic force of a blue moon. Each calendar month, the earth experiences shifts in lunar energy as the moon changes from the birth of a new moon (usually mid-month) to the death of a full moon (usually at the beginning or end of the month). New moon energy provides a gateway to bring new opportunities into our life, whereas full moon energy provides a gateway to release the old. The blue moon on 31st July 2015 was particularly powerful, as it was the second full moon of the month – the first was on 2nd July. This meant that in July, the moon had travelled through one and a half cycles from full, to new, to full again – all in the same month. This only ever happens on rare occasions, hence the saying 'once in a blue moon'. The moon itself appeared to be much closer to earth and much larger than a regular full moon, which made its energetic effects on the body even more powerful. Blue moons are said to bring us in touch with our emotional and inner selves, and they are recognised as an opportunity to let go of past, outdated beliefs in order to make way for a new path. For me, it was an opportunity to finally walk through the pain of my past life and lock the door on my grief once and for all.

I travelled to Ireland with my cousin Barry, his dad – my uncle Paul – and Millie. Fionn stayed behind with Tony's family, as the younger family members weren't going to be attending the wedding. We arrived at the airport with plenty of time to spare and settled down for some lunch, a glass of wine and a good old catch up. We made a pit stop for a quick drink before boarding the plane, all four of us aware of the time but somehow not paying attention to it. When we arrived at the departure gates we thought we had 20 minutes to spare and stood in line, or at least in what we thought was our line. Luton has a small but expanding airport and handles many flights, which mainly depart for European destinations. The holding area for our departure to Dublin was Gate 15 and 16, which by design was not big enough to hold the passengers for two flights leaving at the same time, which appeared to be the case. People were queued up everywhere and the area was very congested. As we joined the queue we asked a lady if this was the line for the Irish flight and she said it was and that she was waiting for the same one. So we stood there thinking nothing of it, failing to realise that the passengers for our flight were being boarded onto the plane and that we were stood in the wrong queue. Don't ask me how four intelligent people could have all made the same mistake, but that's exactly what happened. My uncle was wandering around and not paying attention, my cousin and Millie were both on their phones and equally distracted, and I was lost in the buzz that came from two glasses of wine combined with jetlag from my flight from Thailand. There was no information on the boards or ground staff milling about, and at no point did it register with any of us that we should actually be on the plane, even though it was due to leave in half an hour. It was as if time had stood still and we were in a vacuum. When I finally snapped out of my trance, I looked at the time on my phone and it suddenly registered we had missed our flight. We pushed our way to the front of the queue and watched as our plane taxied off to the runway without us. I was gobsmacked. In all my years of flying I had never once missed a plane, but here we were grounded as our flight left without us. We went back to the ticket desk to discover there were no seats available on any flights to Ireland that day, and the airline only had two seats available the next morning. Shit. My cousin's wedding was in less than 24-hours and we had to get out to Ireland come what may. In that moment of crisis, the four of us dissolved back to our true nature. I immediately went into philosophical fixer mode, taking control and charging off on my white horse to rescue us all, while my cousin was calm and searched the internet for solutions. My uncle went off for a smoke. Meanwhile, Millie sprung onto social media to let everyone know of the impending drama. After an hour of internet searching we came up with the best solution, which was for me to drive five hours to Wales, catch the overnight ferry to Dublin – another four hours – and then drive to southern Ireland – a further two hours. All being well we would arrive at our destination by 10am the next morning. And that was that. A simple one-hour flight being missed had turned into a mammoth road trip, and so much more.

I took another hour or so to get my car back from the car park, and at 3:30pm we headed out of Luton Airport and up the M1 motorway under the steam of our blue moon. I prayed all the way for an easy ride, because Friday afternoons on the M1 motorway are notoriously bad and we didn't have the luxury of time on our side. We had a wedding to attend in 22-hours and counting. But my prayers were answered. The traffic was kind, and as I drove up the motorway we listened to amazing music on BBC Radio 1, which was playing all the classics from top DJs in Ibiza. We laughed, chatted and actually enjoyed our road trip. It was an opportunity to bond, mother and daughter, father and son, but it was also an opportunity to lead by example. I wanted to show my daughter that everything is possible, if we choose to see the blessings in what is. The journey could have so easily been one involving self-blame and frustration, but instead we made it fun. But I also knew that however detached I appeared from any self-recrimination, the universe had given me another lesson in drinking. Let's be clear, one of the factors that made us miss the flight was having that cheeky pit stop at the bar. This threw my senses and made me less focused than normal. It's my truth and I accept that, not with blame, but with appreciation that I am learning my lessons. I'm accepting these lessons and making the changes necessary so that they don't happen again – this is the path to a peaceful life.

We made it to the wedding location exhausted, but with a few hours to spare to freshen up and grab some food. The ceremony itself was very difficult for me. When my beautiful cousin walked down the aisle, I was transported back in time to my own wedding day, to August 2004. As I closed my eyes, I relived that special moment all over again as my heart exploded with waves of longing and sadness. I could see myself gliding down the aisle to meet my beloved at the altar. It was totally surreal, like I was caught in an altered state of reality. I was shocked and overwhelmed by the intensity of my feelings. Every time I thought I had dealt with my grief, the waves of loss, love and passion clawed at my heart in the most unexpected way. I tried to stifle my tears and keep my composure – this was my cousin's special day after all, it wasn't about me – but when Tony's name was mentioned in the Prayers of the Faithful, as is tradition in Irish weddings, I couldn't hold onto my emotions anymore. My heart broke and I cried my eyes out. My mum reached out to comfort me, but I pulled away and whispered to her, "No, please let me be." I no longer wanted to hold onto the tears. I wanted to sit with the sorrow knowing that I was finally giving it space to pass. It was desperately hard to watch two people as in love as Tony and I had been starting off on their lives together with so much anticipation and passion. Here I was feeling the same sense of love that I felt on my own wedding day, as my soul was transported back in time. It was indescribable. But somehow I knew it was life's way of telling me that love never dies. Tony's love was still there for me, even though the white wings of death had carried him away. His physical body may have left this earth, but the love I had for my husband lived on in my heart. And it was now time to give that love to me. The song of love and marriage is perhaps best told through the exquisite poem in the *The Prophet* by Kahlil Gibran

> *"Then Almitra spoke again and said, 'And what of marriage master?'*
>
> *And he answered, saying:*
>
> *'You were born together and together you shall be for evermore.*
>
> *You shall be together when the white wings of death scatter your days.*
>
> *Aye, you shall be together even in the silent memory of God.*
>
> *But let there be spaces in your togetherness.*
>
> *And let the winds of heaven dance between you.*
>
> *Love one another, but make not a bond of love:*
>
> *Let it rather be a moving sea between the shores of your souls.*
>
> *Fill each other's cup but drink not from one cup.*

Give one another of your bread but eat not from the same loaf.

Sing and dance together and be joyous, but let each one of you be alone.

Even as the strings of a lute are alone though they quiver with the same music.

Give your hearts, but not into each other's keeping.

And stand together yet not too near together:

For the pillars of the temple stand apart,

And the oak tree and the cypress grow not in each other's shadow.'"

The wedding breakfast was long and boozy and everyone dined out on the story about us missing the flight. In a moment of seriousness I said I thought it was divine intervention and was down to the blue moon's energy. The guests at my table were stunned by this and clearly thought I had gone insane. Lesson to self: it's not easy being a lone voice when it comes to defending spiritual matters, and sometimes it's best to keep my views safely to myself! But I didn't let other people's attempts to ridicule me affect my peace. There was a time when I would have fought fiercely to win an argument, but now I accept that another person's view can't affect my state of being, so it really doesn't matter if my family think I'm slightly nuts – it's what I think that counts.

By 9pm, I'd hit the wall and had had enough. I felt almost flu-like with exhaustion. I managed to sneak away in the interval after the meal, just before the dancing and real partying began, and went to my room for a nap. I drifted off to sleep and didn't wake again until 4am, by which point I'd missed the entire party. I wasn't upset or disappointed, as the whole weekend felt very much out of my control. The next morning I said my farewells and took the long drive home back to England, this time on my own, as Millie, Paul and Barry took the return flight back to Luton. I cried, screamed and shouted into the air as I released the pain of the past and fought with my will to hold on. I was so depressed, angry and plain fed up with life that I knew I had to make some big changes. It was time. And so, when I asked myself again what it was that I wanted, I didn't draw a blank. This time, the answer came in the beautiful words of Nayyirah Waheed[23]

"Eyes that commit
That is what I am looking for"

I wanted to find love again. And I knew the path to love started with me.

The third chakra is called Manipura, which means jewelled city. Manipur is a state in North-Eastern India that is famed for its beauty and fine golden silk thread, which is unique to the region. The chakra is located at the solar plexus, around the naval region, and is concerned with generating fire in the body. The fire of the sun feeds the fire of our will and when the third chakra is in balance, the body has vital energy to put true desires into action. Manipura is the powerhouse of our system. Without a strong will, we don't have the fire to manifest and we become stuck in lower level childlike consciousness. It was clear to me now that my fire needed feeding. My will was depleted and I'd become stuck in time, stuck in my widow story and stuck in St Albans. I was being called to step into my beauty and to stop hiding behind my sorrow. I had sat in the safety of my house in St Albans for too long. I actually felt as if it had wrapped its arms around me and protected me for many years. This was the house that Tony and Dad built for me and it held my heart, but now it was time to release it somehow. I had this sense that if I sold up and moved somewhere new I could finally move on. So I put the house up for sale. The trouble was, not one single person showed an interest in buying it. Not one. It was completely baffling. My house is the most beautiful one on my road, it's in the most desirable area of St Albans and it's near the best schools and road links. The estate agents couldn't work out what was going on and neither could I. I left the house on the market for four months and received very little interest, eventually taking the 'for sale' sign down at the end of the summer. It was clear the house didn't want to be sold. It had other plans for me.

> *"A truth which comes to us from without bears ever the stamp of uncertainty. Conviction attaches only to what appears as truth to each of us in our own heart."* [24]

So I sat with it and listened to my heart. I focused on what I wanted in my daily meditation and kept coming back to this need to have a stronger sense of self. I had to step out of the comfort zone of who I used to be and discover who I was now. And this was the work of the third chakra, and the process of individuation, which, in Jungian psychology, concerns stepping out of the unconscious behaviour that allows us to be defined by others, such as our cultural conditioning and our parental influences, and stepping into our own space. It's about having the strength to say, "This is who I am" and not to be defined by others and where you came from. And that takes strength, courage and fire. For me, this was about cutting attachment to my Catholic faith and stepping further into my truth and my heart. To do this I had to step into my power. It meant taking my son out of the Catholic education system and putting him into a Rudolf Steiner school, where the philosophy is to develop free, morally responsible, integrated individuals. Steiner schools feed the mind, body and soul of the child, and this is what I wanted for Fionn. It was another step out of the system and towards a new life. By leaving my job at the BBC, I'd already turned my back on the corporate world and I'd also made a conscious decision to be vegetarian and only eat sustainably-sourced, fresh organic food. I was committed to my energy work and meditation, and I had planted the seed to live somewhere else that was better suited to my new way of being. I knew I was evolving and growing, but it took vast amounts of courage and energy to stand my ground, especially as I was stepping into the unknown and I felt very depleted and tired all the time. Up to this point in my life, I had pretty much lived a life of compliance, as I'd conformed to the wishes of others and the direction of our family way. Through the work on my first and second chakra, I could now see that my own inner power, my third chakra, was just as deficient as my mother's, and this resulted in my passive aggressive behaviour.

Part of the work of healing a deficient third chakra is through exercise and nutrition. Doing the right type of exercise that leaves you feeling energized and full of vitality is an essential ingredient to fuelling the fires of the core. I'm no stranger to this through my yoga practice, but over the years, I have adapted my practice to bring more breath and awareness to my solar plexus, which has helped to strengthen my will. And I've become more mindful about nutrition and moved towards a conscious diet supplemented with good plant based superfoods, such as bee pollen, cacao, hemp and spirulina. I ensure I drink plenty of water throughout the day, but just as importantly I avoid drinking water 30 minutes before a meal as this over saturates the digestive system and dilutes the enzymes which are needed to efficiently turn food into fuel. It's a simple but effective method to improve digestion.

Being comfortable at expressing anger is also very much the domain of third chakra healing. When anger isn't expressed at the appropriate time it's often redirected towards our nearest and dearest.

"Releasing anger about our father keeps us from continually badgering our husbands or boyfriends. Standing up to our mothers keeps us from resenting our wives, girlfriends or daughters." [25]

This fact was a bit of a revelation to me, especially with regards to my relationship with my teenage daughter. When we heal the karma of our past, we are less likely to bring this negative energy into the relationships in our present. I knew that I needed to do the work and heal the wounds of the mother/child bond. But as I mothered my inner child and showed her compassion and forgiveness, and at the same time put healthy boundaries around my relationship with my mother, I noticed that my relationship with my daughter also started to improve. It was quite phenomenal. Our daily interactions went from being a constant slanging match to one of relative (I use that word loosely!) peace and harmony. And as I witnessed this in my home, it opened my eyes yet again to the connectivity of everything in my world. The people around us always give us an opportunity to improve ourselves.

"It pays to plan ahead. It wasn't raining when Noah built the ark."

And finally, to heal the third chakra deficiency, you've got to have a plan. Now you'd think someone like me who headed up a planning team at the BBC for over a decade would have had this one licked, but in truth, when Tony died, I stopped making plans. I lost all faith in life for a while and couldn't find any joy in planning anything on my own. But I knew the value of goal setting and visualisation, and when I did set goals, I always achieved them. Always. Every time. So rather tentatively, I set out to ask myself what I wanted, and by the end of the summer there were things I was absolutely certain about. One was that I was going to be an internationally acclaimed bestselling author, and that this book would go out to the world and help people on a grand scale. And the second was I wanted to find love. I wanted to find a beautiful enduring romantic love with a special man who would love me for who I am now. This is what I wanted and through healing the third chakra, I was at last opening the doorway to receiving these blessings

11

Dealing With Depression

"The feeling associated with giving up something loved – or at least something that is part of ourselves and familiar – is depression."[26]

I needed to ride through the waves of depression once and for all to release my heart from the grip of grief and open it to the possibility of love. I was fed up with spending night after night on my own. I wanted someone beautiful to lay their head on my pillow and kiss me goodnight. I wanted to wake up in their arms in the morning knowing they would be there again for me the next night. I was done with the loneliness and the boredom and I wanted to spend my life with someone who shared my dreams and visions. I had done the work of balancing the lower chakras and now I wanted to heal my heart and welcome in a new love. My beautiful soul sister, Alex, told me how she'd written a letter to the universe as a way of manifesting love – and then she'd met her wonderful husband, Dan. And the wonderful Wayne Dyer always used to stress the importance of writing things down when we want to manifest our dreams. When we write down our wishes, we are making a contract with the universe, so we need to be very specific about what it is we want. This is why it is so important to strengthen the will and do the work of the third chakra, because we can't *ask* for what we want if we don't *know* what we want. As I wrote my letter to the universe, I sealed it with love and put it in my visualisation box along with crystals, images and words of everything I wanted to manifest in my life. I even slipped a picture of George Clooney in there for the hell of it – you can't blame a girl for trying! And then I let it be, and I got on with the job of healing my heart. My letter read:

Dear Universe

I am so grateful for the beautiful children and wonderful friends that have blessed my life. I am ready to meet a wonderful man to share my life with. I want a man who is kind and beautiful in spirit. Someone who wants to be the best they can in this world, and who shares the same values as me. I want him to be ambitious but also philanthropic, caring for the world and the people around him by actively showing support for environmental causes. He must be intelligent, with a good sense of humour, and handsome. I want a man who cares for himself in both a physical and an emotional way – someone who knows his own mind. He needs to be true and honest, but also open, generous and warm to those who are close to him. I want him to love me without question, with passion and desire. I want him to treat my children as if they were his own and be a fabulous influence in their lives, showing them kindness and compassion through his own actions.

And I want to love my new man with all my heart. I want him to be important to me, but not as important as I am to myself. I want to laugh lots, have fun, experience new adventures and make love often. I want our relationship to be easy, as if we were made for each other, so that when we meet we will just know.

I trust in the divine universe in me to honour the love I can see.

With blessings, Dee xx

The fourth chakra is called Anahata and it is located at the heart centre, which is the seat of universal love. Individual consciousness is developed through the lower chakras when we define our being, and collective consciousness is developed through the higher chakras. These serve to expand the self. However, it is love that sits at the heart of the chakra system and helps to redeem us to infinity.

"How do you spell love?" asked Piglet
"You don't spell it, you feel it," – said Pooh

A.A Milne

And love opens with feelings. When the heart is open we can access and feel the beauty of it in everything. We are able to enjoy wonderful relationships and intimacy with a partner, as well as bathe the soul in the light of self-love. This is the gift of a balanced heart chakra. But for many people, the heart suffers from wounds, which means it is shut down from the magic of love and fearful as a result of rejection and suffering. For me, the work of healing the heart chakra was very much rooted in self-love. This is because I'm a classic codependent, so I tend to fixate on others and give everything to everyone else, leaving myself empty. There are very few people who reach middle age without suffering from some sort of wound to the heart, be it through divorce, grief, or through some other form of loss. And it's likely we will move through periods when the heart is open, such as when we fall in love or have children and experience the full joy of life, but we will also go through periods when the heart is closed – and these are the times when we are faced with loss or rejection.

In Jungian psychotherapy[27], the process of individuation continues with the marriage of the internal female and male archetypes, which are known as the anima and animus. We are made up of a mix of both male and female energy, and we tend to carry the complementary characteristics to our physical body. So women have the traits of a more masculine soul and men have the traits of a more feminine one. Outwardly, women are more nurturing and feeling, but inwardly they are more logical and reflective. On the other hand, men are outwardly more logical and objective, yet inwardly it is the man who feels. This is why men are more vulnerable to despair, whereas women are more capable of finding hope and comfort. This translates into statistics when we look at things like suicide rates: men are twice as likely to take their own lives as women are. And in premature babies, boys often fare worse than girls.

Just as the Shadow Self can be projected onto others in a relationship if it is not owned and integrated, so too can the characteristics of the anima and animus. So, if a woman does not own the masculine characteristic that she sees in the cultural stereotype of the perfect male – such as strength, power and chivalry, then she projects these romanticised states onto her male relationships, which gives the man very little room to hide from his obvious faults. Unless he's George Clooney, of course! And if a man doesn't own his own feminine side he may well project an idealised female nature onto his partner, which could be an overly passive or sexualised version of the modern independent women. By balancing male and female energy we can enter into relationships with the opposite sex with more realistic expectations and a freedom to show our true self. This has become more essential in modern society, where women are taking on traditional male roles in the work place and divorce rates are skyrocketing. I believe this has to do with our persona and our social identity. Social identity is the ideal picture of ourselves that we present to the world. So, if we hold ourselves up as the brave, powerful male hero, or the good, obedient girl, we set about creating relationships based on this idealised image of who we are. But, as we discovered in the work of the shadow through the second chakra, we are more than just the persona. The self is made up of the conscious and unconscious mind, and to become whole and evolve as a being we need to integrate the shadow and the persona, as well as other archetypes, into the self. The anima and animus hold the collective consciousness of what it means to be male and female, and it is highly influenced by our culture, our parents and by mythology. This is why women marry men who are just like their fathers. The way we relate to our internalised female and male energy comes from how we were treated as children by our parents. It'll therefore be no surprise for you to learn that most of my male partners have had issues with addiction, just as my own father did, or that I inherited issues concerning denial and control from my mother. This imprint from our primary carers runs deep and influences how we communicate with the world. The archetypal female from mythology and religion also influences us. The universal mother has appeared in the myths and stories of our ancestors as the goddess, the semi mortal, the hero and the demon, to name just a few. Jung observed that it's these archetypes that appear to us in our dreams and fantasies. However, over time we have become more separated from the knowledge and wisdom of the mother, especially in the West. We operate in a modern system that is highly individualised and is orientated around material value. The inner value of human love has been forgotten in the mainstream, and we have lost touch with the nurturing embrace of the divine female. Instead, we have lived under the rule of dominant masculine energy, which is characteristically powerful and strong, but also divisive. And our beautiful planet is hurting because of it. I truly believe we all need to step into our inner goddess and embrace a new way of being where the female takes a more active role in influencing the world.

There are many ways in which we can become more in touch with the divine feminine, and one of the easiest ones is to listen to your heart. Let your heart be the guide that shines the light on everything you do. Listen to it, feel it. Honour thy heart and it will honour you back. When something feels right, your heart will show you its truth through the sensations and energy it sends out to the body. The magic begins when we get out of our thinking masculine mind and into our feeling feminine heart.

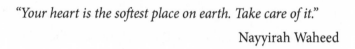

"Your heart is the softest place on earth. Take care of it."

Nayyirah Waheed

It's not possible to have love without loss. This fact is one of the greatest struggles of the heart. And the balance between the need to attach and be free is a very delicate one. We must accept that to experience great love, we will also discover great sorrow and grief. The two walk together hand in hand. And the expansion of the heart comes from both sides of the dance. It doesn't mean that all relationships will end in doom and gloom, what it means is we need to have a healthy appreciation that the heart's desire to attach in relationships is just as strong as the soul's desire to be free. This was powerful learning for me. In my relationships, I have always been very consumed by my man of the moment. The type of men I used to date always seemed to want my constant attention, as much as I expected theirs. But now I had a new framework of understanding that gave me an opportunity to really think about what I wanted from a romantic union. I had dined out on the notion of romantic love for years. The idea of boy meets girl and falls in love and lives happily ever after. But the work of the heart chakra had prepared me for another way.

> *"The heart chakra is about bonding. Unintegrated parts of ourselves that are not bonded into the heart with love will seek bonding elsewhere."* [28]

And the truth is we bring into our world the parts of ourselves that we are not willing to see. So the anger that I failed to own for so long came back at me through my daughter's fiery temper. And so did my depression. I was unaware that my soul was deeply depressed; my denial of the depths of my grief and my insistence that I had ridden the wave and was OK clung to me. But I couldn't avoid what my outer world was showing me. I was surrounded by people who were, for many different reasons, suffering from depression. They seemed to come to me for comfort, and I couldn't ignore the fact that mental health problems were something that ran deep in our family wound. My father had bouts of depression spurned on, no doubt, by excessive drinking. Although alcohol gives people an initial buzz, depression is one of the key side effects when it starts to leave the body. This is why I suffer so badly if I drink, because it brings darkness with it and forces me to face the demon of depression.

But the single most significant discovery that helped me bring my fourth chakra into balance happened when I had a soul vibrational reading in late August. By then I was accustomed to tarot readings and found them absolutely fascinating. I couldn't quite believe how accurately my readings reflected my life, and to be honest the male logical soul in me had always denied this type of esoteric practice as a load of old mumbo jumbo. But as I opened to spirit and the angelic realm, I actually started to find the guidance highly beneficial, although I wasn't always ready to listen! But in August 2015, I stepped inside a shop called Destiny Rising in Hertfordshire and I met Mandy. And she blew my mind. She knew nothing about me, but, as she tuned into me energetically, she told me everything I needed to know.

She said that my main issue was control. I wasn't allowing life to flow and I was holding on. She talked about my mother and how she was in denial, was fearful of this world and didn't want to see beyond what her eyes told her. But she wasn't talking about my mother, she was talking about me, and my internalised mother archetype. She sensed my inner pain and her body contorted as she told me I had too much heartache from past love. She said I was exhausted from it all and it was draining me almost to the point where I had ME.

Then she said, "Dee, you have to stop associating pain with love. Love does not feel like this."

And that's when it really hit home. And she was absolutely bloody right. I had built this fantasy bond around my need to be loved, and I'd projected it into my relationship with The Big Guy. My denial of my childhood experience had carried itself into adulthood and I'd developed a very warped sense of what love was. Understanding this had a profound effect on me, as it allowed me to see that my relationship choices were driven by a false sense of love. I became aware that I had an opportunity to heal the pains of the mother.

"Since the need for love is so strong in the excessive heart chakra, there may be poor boundaries and poor discrimination. We may fail to discern when a relationship becomes abusive and live in the fantasy bond where everything is just fine." [29]

The arms are an extension of the heart, and when the arms are weak and limp the heart is closed and afraid. When the heart is open the arms and hands are open to receive life. It was one of the first things I noticed about Tony – he used to walk around with his fists clenched. I remember saying to him, "What are you holding onto, darling?" I didn't realise it at the time, but it was me who really needed to hear those words. We open our arms and hearts to receive in yoga through backbending, which I bloody hated. Everything used to hurt when I did backbends: my arms, my shoulders and my spine. But I knew I had to go into the pain to come out the other side, so I started to tweak my yoga practice and focused on opening my heart. There were times when I left my mat sobbing, and other times when I thought I would stop breathing altogether. But as the fire and will in me grew stronger, as I worked through my third chakra, I had more determination than ever before and felt a willingness to face whatever lay in the stillness of the pose.

If you do not have a regular yoga practice, but want to work on opening your heart, a safe way to do this is to lie down on your back supported by a cushion under your spine. You can then bend your knees or keep them straight – whatever is more comfortable. Open your arms so that they rest on the ground at shoulder height, and your body is in a T shape. Now just be. Stay in this position for up to 10 minutes, or longer if you are comfortable, and resist the temptation to move unless you feel real discomfort (then, of course, you must readjust yourself). As you allow the body to settle, observe the sensations of the breath as you relax into this submissive position in order to receive. Try not to fight any feelings or sensations that come your way. Be gentle and kind to yourself. When it's time to come out, roll gently onto your right-hand side and stay there for a few more moments as you blink your eyes open and bring awareness back to the whole self.

I also did a lot of shamanic journeying and sound energy work, as I stepped into my heart's desire and let the beat of the drum and the gong carry my soul away. A shamanic journey is a spiritual tradition where the participant accesses the help of their spirit guide, as part of their soul leaves the body and goes on a journey with them. Journeying is usually done to the beat of a drum, and the rhythm of the drum allows the soul to wander – similar to when one is in a dream state. My journeys have always taken me over a bridge in India, with someone magical waiting for me on the other side. I found that bridge a year later. It is the most delightful bridge I have ever seen and it crosses the Talpona River in Southern Goa. And it was when I reached India – the motherland – that I started to do the *real* work of healing the Mother archetype, as I stepped into my divine feminine power and journeyed into the womb to find my inner goddess.

And so, life moved on as I started to listen to my heart's desires. I became increasingly aware that I no longer wanted to live my middle-class suburban dream in St Albans. It just felt like that didn't fit me anymore, but I had no idea what the alternative was. As I pondered on my future, Fionn and I enjoyed the last few days of the school summer holidays in beautiful Swanage, a small seaside fishing village nestled in the Isle of Purbeck in Dorset – a place that has a magical, romantic, unspoilt energy to it. It is home to lots of artists and creative folk, and we stayed with my dear friend Connie, chilling out and soaking up the earthiness of our surroundings. We went for walks on the beach, swam in the sea and wandered in the countryside, doing our best to dodge the intermittent bursts of rain typical of a British summertime.

"Sit in the ocean. It is one of the best medicines on the planet" [30]

I was starting to find great appreciation in the simple things in life, such as days out with friends, playing by the river and having easy, uncomplicated fun. This was something that had been missing from my life for so long. I felt like I finally had the energy to give my beautiful son the love and attention he needed. Previously, I'd been battling with my grief so much that I'd struggled to do this. It was hard enough to get through the days, let alone muster up anything extra. But as I started to spring back to life,. I realised that my heart was screaming out for fresh air and fun. I needed the outdoor life. I thought long and hard about what it was that made me so happy and passionate about life when I travelled. My passion was fed by visiting new places, meeting new people, experiencing new cultures and eating amazing foods, but it was also about being outside in nature. I loved being by the ocean or in the mountains or the desert – anywhere that isn't contained within four concrete walls. I had this strong desire to want to feel it all again. I longed to feel the wind in my hair, the rain down my back, the sand between my toes and the sun on my face. It was like I needed to feed my soul with the elements. I was done with being stuck inside the protective four walls of my house, now I wanted to be outside and living. I knew I needed to go elsewhere to find my peace, I just didn't know where to go.

"If you always do what you always did,
you will always get what you always got."
Albert Einstein

As the long lazy days of summer drew to a close, I also started to question what type of relationship I wanted in the future. I had put my intentions out in my letter to the universe, but I still wasn't sure what I wanted from a man. Challenging all my preconceived ideas about marriage and love certainly made for an interesting time. Up to that point in my life, I had only ever dated English or Irish guys who were always a few years older and normally tall, giants of men who fitted my template of being nice looking, funny and reasonably smart – I use that term loosely for some of them! But I suddenly realised how dull that was making me sound. It's like sticking your hand in the sweetie jar and only ever picking the orange cream when there's a whole host of exciting possibilities out there. It was time to reprogram my thinking. I knew I wanted to meet someone who was completely different. If I'm honest, my taste in men had been somewhat questionable! I often entered into relationships consciously thinking: *What on earth am I doing here with this guy?* But the strong need to attach often dominated my senses, and I know I stayed way longer than was healthy in some relationships so I could feed my desire to fix others. Thankfully, through working on myself, I know I'm no longer like that. Whoever comes into my life next will be there for all the right reasons. It was time to step into my truth and live a life worth living.

12 Facing The Fear

There are 69 acronyms for fear on Google. I've listed a few of my favourites below, but they all have a common theme, and that is the ability to accept and deal with *what is*.

Fuck Everything And Run – This is my favourite!
For Everything A Reason
Frantic Effort to Avoid Reality
Forever Escaping And Retreating
Failure Expected And Received
Finding Excuses And Reasons

Fear is the great divider of humanity. Anything that is fear based keeps us separate from our true self and from each other. Fear is always the ego at play, the monkey mind telling us we can't, or shouldn't, or aren't able to, or we don't have enough (you can fill in the gap) time, money, energy, etc. Or we can't possibly do it this way, or whatever the exhaustive story our mind wants to invent to keep us stuck in a place of darkness.

And when we put it like that, living with fear is pretty damn unappealing, but we all do it at some point in our lives. We all stay stuck or limit ourselves because we are too afraid of the unknown. I remember this feeling only too well from my school days. I was always the girl on the outside looking in. I was so frightened of rejection that I never put myself out there with the 'in crowd', although they would have happily welcomed me in. The limitation was mine, not theirs. I was always doing something else, but not really doing anything at all. And when it came to my options and the subjects to study for my A Levels, I distinctly remember picking the ones that made sense, and the ones my teachers wanted me to do, over the ones that my heart was crying out to do. And my heart wanted to write and study English literature. My heart wanted to devour the books of Shakespeare and write beautiful stories. I remember my English teacher at the time reading a verse from Romeo and Juliet and asking the class if anyone knew the significance of the piece. He said if we understand the depth of this piece we should really study English. Nobody put their hand up, but I knew. I knew the answer. I knew the verse he read was a soliloquy, which is a speech the character says to themselves that highlights their inner thoughts and feelings. I knew it because my inner voice was saying to me, "Dee, you love English you want to study literature and become a great writer. Put your hand up."

Writing was all I ever wanted to do. But my monkey mind said, *"Who do you think you are? If the people around you don't know how could you possibly know?"*

And so I was too afraid to admit it. I sat with it and I shrivelled in my seat when he revealed the answer because it was another lost moment for me to shine. I didn't go on to study English; I took statistics, economics, and geography, which led me down a career path in media and business. It wasn't what my heart wanted but thank God I followed a reasonably creative route and didn't go with the careers advisor's top recommendation, which was a job as an actuary! Gulp!

My life after that was littered with many moments when I was too afraid to show myself. I remember walking away from many business meetings wishing I'd had the courage to say what I really wanted to say. And the nagging voice of recrimination usually came to me at the end of the day when I was in bed, as I chewed over the events of the day and the silent voice in my head would say, *"Dee, why didn't you say x, y or z?"* It happened a lot when I worked at the BBC. There were lots of 'big' voices there and endless hours of debate. I used to say that an attempt to make a decision at the BBC was akin to the start of a good conversation. Everybody had an opinion and they all wanted to have their say.

"Understand me.
I'm not like an ordinary world.
I have my madness,
I live in another dimension
and I do not have time for things
that have no soul."

Charles Bukowski

I first heard my inner voice in November 2011, when I had a life coaching session with an acquaintance whom was starting a new business and wanted to try out some techniques on me. She asked me to imagine I was 75 and sitting on my rocking chair reminiscing about my life…the one I had already and the one that was yet to come. She gave me five-minutes to sit quietly and write everything down. Here's what I wrote:

"Well, I'm not 75, I'm 85, and I'm sitting in my penthouse in New York overlooking Central Park. I then joked that I was having an affair with the bellboy downstairs, 20 years younger than me. We roared laughing as I imagined myself with the same glint in my eye and desire for fun and sex as I have now. But be careful what you wish!

I am a well-known writer, I've been on television in America and I've acted in a few plays on Broadway.

I'm desperately proud of my two children who are extremely successful in their own right. Millie is working in film and Fionn is a bright light in his field. I have a passion for travel and have continued to visit many countries through my charitable efforts. I have helped build a school in India

Both my children have married well and are extremely happy. I have six wonderful grandchildren. I feel immensely proud to have been Tony's wife and still feel his love in my heart.

I have met and married an even greater love, who was my soul companion and the love of my life, and we were extremely happy together.

I have a PhD and I am grateful for my health and the wonderful circle of friends I've remained close to throughout my life."

I remember looking down at the list and saying to my acquaintance, "Oh my God, yoga doesn't even feature here." This seemed strange at the time because I was just beginning to embark on a new life as a yoga teacher. But on reflection, something deep inside always knew that my path as a yoga teacher was only ever given to heal me. I came to yoga for the purest of reasons, to heal myself, but it has also given me so much more. It has given me the protective guiding lights of my soul sisters, Jennifer and Alex, and an amazing friendship with my teacher Taran.

Four years after writing my reflections at 85, I sat down to write this, my first book.

It seemed like 2015 was going to be one of those years. On 27th September, the world witnessed another significant lunar event when a super blood moon and lunar eclipse blessed the earth. It brought with it another energetic gateway and the promise of transformational change. By sheer luck, I attended a yoga workshop in London called, "Facing the fear on and off the matt." This was led by a beautifully instinctive teacher, who is very in tune with energy work. She was also honest enough to admit the timing of the workshop was purely a scheduling coincidence, although I've come to realise there are no coincidences in life, so I believe it must have been divine intervention at play. This was the week when the heavens opened to shift blocks from the past that were rooted in fear. The essential message from the workshop was that we needed to get out of the mind space that constantly says, "I can't" and go into the heart space which says, "Yes you can". And this is exactly what we do when we balance the fourth chakra – we open up the possibilities of the heart. Fear keeps us in the head space, a space of questioning, anxiety, worry and lack, and out of the heart space, which is where our real desires are.

The teacher described the moment of moving out of fear as the moment of integration. It's the moment of awareness where we say, "I can" and also *feel* we can. It's the moment in a handstand when the fear of falling stops you from getting to the top, but you say, "I'm going to get to the top and do it anyway, and so what if I fall, I can always get up and try again." It's the moment the body releases any effort and softens into the pose. If you practice yoga you will understand this feeling. It is the feeling that you are the pose. You are not in it. It is in you. It feels graceful, effortless and fearless. The point of integration is where the mind and heart come together as one. It's that split second when the mind stops controlling – there's that word again – and the union takes place to achieve the heart's desires. It is where all the ground work and will of the lower chakras meets the effortlessness energy of the higher ones.

This heart opening integration happened to me in the very last pose, when I dropped into a very deep backbend. My friend Alex was with me and she kept saying, "Just do it, Dee, you can do it." And at that moment, spurred on by her loving encouragement, I said, "Fuck it" and completely let go. I flew back and I did it. I fell back from Ustrasana (camel) to Urdhva Dhanurasana (full wheel) and marvelled at my body's capability to go beyond the limits of my mind. I felt so empowered, because I knew at that moment I'd stepped off my "I can't do" attitude and into my "I can do" way of being, which is where I live now. I stepped into a place where I suddenly believed everything was possible, a place where I saw the body as a vehicle to serve the soul and could finally release the fear that was hidden deep within. I learnt three very profound lessons from that workshop about the nature of fear.

You have to face fear full on in order to move forward in life.

Fear hides behind a story, and *the story is a way of disguising our fear.*

By releasing fear, we get to see the true self.

The thing with fear is, when we face small challenges and rise above them, we build confidence and belief in life. It's as if we boost our internal bank of courage, making us more prepared for when we have to deal with the really difficult things in life. But if we never go to this place…if we only ever stay in our comfort zone and play things safe, we'll lack the skills and bravery to face the big stuff when it comes our way, such as sudden death, illness, redundancy or divorce. So my advice is, don't live life in the slipstream, every now and again go out and do something that scares the life out of you, and don't hide under the duvet when you next see a spider, unless it's poisonous , then I suggest you run!

Another thing that fear teaches us is that it is OK to not always have the answer. It teaches us to get comfortable with the unknown. The greatest inventions and achievements in life never end up as they were originally intended. That's why they're great, because they kept evolving and changing to become better. They didn't stay stuck. When we get comfortable with the unknown, the outcome is usually far greater than what our small, limited minds could ever have expected.

Fear also teaches us about the stories we weave around our lives and the excuses we make because we're too scared to make changes. The workshop helped me see that I had been hiding out in my widow story for way too long, and it masked my real fear, which was the fear of the unknown; the fear of life itself. It was time to stop trying to control life and to move to a place of absolute trust, where I could let go of attachment and learn to live in the flow.

Autumn 2015

By autumn I had reached the point of no return. I was in transition and was being prepared for a new life. I had made peace with my childhood and, through the work of the lower chakras, was beginning to think about my future and what I wanted from life. I had sent my letter out to the universe and was opening my heart to the divine feminine energy within. Through balancing the heart chakra, I had also opened up to the possibility of love. Now it was time to step into the higher chakras and into the divine wisdom of universal consciousness. I viewed harvest time as a chance to take stock and show gratitude for the blessing that had helped me to get to this point in my life.

It was time to prepare for my new life and do the work to leave the old one behind. It was time to open my ears and eyes to a new way of being through the work of balancing the fifth and sixth chakras. It was an opportunity to hear the internal voice within, to open up to the power of the third eye and my natural intuition, and to recognise the archetypal energy that was guiding my life and showing me what I needed to do to realise my dreams. In late October 2015, I spent a blissful week on a juicing retreat in Turkey and enjoyed the pleasure of solitude for the first time in my adult life since the children were born. I took time out of my daily life to reflect, rest and just be. It was heaven and I was able to see all the wonders of my life and appreciate the lessons I had learnt from my two magical children. I thought about my warrior child, Millie, whose passion and determination to fight for a better world is fierce and honourable. I also thought about my angel child, Fionn, whose wisdom and compassion has always astounded me. My children helped me heal by reflecting back to me my own weaknesses. It was my love for them and my ability to finally see their anger, frustration and wisdom *as an extension of my own* that helped me heal the wounds that lingered in my soul. Healing the mother/child bond was about stepping into a place where I no longer felt attached to my suffering. It was the lesson I needed to learn from the third noble truth, which is, "Suffering ceases when attachment to desire ceases." That day came when my daughter within released me from the chains of disapproval and criticism and said, "Go out into the world and be the strongest, most courageous, most beautiful woman that I know you are." I will remember that day forever because it was the day I truly felt free.

And so the Autumn of 2015 provided the gateway to a new me. At times I struggled and clung onto the past, and at times I could see clearly and forged forward fearlessly with my plans. Along the way I was graced with these valuable lessons:

- ***Our children are our greatest teachers***. Listen to your children. They share so much wisdom in their childlike tantrums and in their innocence to see the truth.
- ***When we detach from desires we will no longer suffer***. Don't be discouraged if things don't seem to go your way. Just keep on moving forward and don't stop. When you know what you want the universe will give it to you at the right time. Let go of control.
- ***In order to understand our patterns and behaviours we need to recognise the sacred archetypal energies.*** As we open the third eye, we start to recognise the patterns and beliefs that form our unconscious subroutines, and we have a means of comprehending them by understanding the influence of archetypal energy.
- ***We need to know that love heals all wounds.*** My purpose in life is to love and to be loved. I believe we are all bound by the one ultimate task and that is to be loved. When we heal our wounds and be ourselves

we open up to the divine grace of love and become a bright beacon that shines this light on the world around us.

13

Finding My Voice

"With sound we are given the power to create from within ourselves using the same primordial energies that create the world around us, and indeed our very selves."[31]

The fifth chakra is called Vissudha in Sanskrit and this means purification. It is located in the throat region, which is the seat of divine communication. By balancing the throat chakra, one learns to speak and hear their truth. It is where we hear the voice of the soul. And my throat had been well and truly blocked for years – blocked in its denial to hear the truth and blocked by fear. I knew deep down, as we always do, what was right for me. I knew about my lessons with alcohol, I knew about my desire to write, I knew about my ambition to live abroad and travel. My life was rooted in the creative arts and was one that was worth living. I'd always known this – I just needed that final push to manifest it. By

Autumn 2015, I was finally able to face the lies I was telling myself by hiding out in this notion that everything was OK and I was happy. I wasn't happy – how can you be when where you are and what you are doing is so far away from where you should be? Lies are the demon of the fifth chakra and I was used to lying to myself because of my codependency habits and my tendency to want to people please. It was all part of the wound of not standing my ground and always putting others first. But I was ready to change all this and had paved the way with my previous work on the lower chakras. Now it was time to open to the voice within to help me see what it was I needed to do in order to make my dreams a reality. This physical voice is the embodiment of the fifth chakra, and the tone and the sound of our voice is a good indicator of how we are feeling on the inside. If the chakra is deficient, the voice will be limited or constricted, sounding almost small and unclear. If the chakra is excessive, the voice may be loud and the person may have a tendency to dominate conversations or constantly interrupt others. A healthy, balanced fifth chakra is one that can express its true self through a balanced mind and body. The voice flows rhythmically and honestly, and it speaks with truth and integrity. It's not afraid to let itself be heard.

The throat is the bridge between the masculine mind and feminine heart. Many women experience issues in this area, as our voices have been silenced throughout the ages by male repression and the church, which was suspicious of our sacred powers. The persecution of women goes back to the story of creation, where Eve is tempted to take the forbidden fruit by the snake, which represents the devil, thus bringing original sin to Adam and man. This idea of the woman and the serpent as 'sinners' doesn't appear in any other mythologies, because the literal translation of the creation story, is not, I believe, how it was meant to be received. The serpent is a metaphor for life itself and is associated with Mother Earth and the goddess. Snakes have the capacity to shed their skin to allow for further growth. The skin dies and transformation happens. The serpent is bound to earth, to the female, to the mother of creativity, and the eagle is bound to the sky, to the male and to spirituality. And this image of conflict between the serpent and the eagle, which has appeared in mythological imagery throughout all cultures and times, represents the conflict between man and woman, the conflict of opposites. But when the two opposites join, we get a magical dragon, a serpent with wings, who is powerful and the hero in many tales. Before Adam and Eve took a bite from the apple, they didn't see themselves as separate. They saw themselves as the same – as one. But when they eat the apple, which represents duality, they discover they are different, and it's this 'difference' that opens them to a world of opposites and to a world of shame. This concept has carried through to how most people experience the world today. Most of us experience life as dualist, with me and you, truth and untruth, good and evil, etc. In my opinion, this is not what the Bible intended with the story of creation. I actually think it was trying to tell us that we are all one. It was teaching us about unity consciousness, and about our connection to nature through life and death. It was the universe that was trying to teach me about life through the story of Martyn, Tony and Paul, but first I had to focus on continuing to heal mySelf. I realised I could do this by observing my children.

Over the years my body had shown me that my fifth chakra was out of balance. I had regular bouts of laryngitis, which literally shut me down for weeks and forced me to listen to the quiet voice within. I also had an excessive fifth chakra, which meant I had a tendency to talk too much. It was my way of masking the emptiness inside. I often interrupted people in my eagerness to show love, and regularly drew the conversation back to myself when someone was talking to me. For example, if one of my girlfriends was telling me about a problem with their boyfriend, I couldn't just listen to them and be empathetic, I always felt compelled to turn the conversation back to me and show solidarity by talking about how I had experienced the same issue. It was as if their problems gave me a platform to air my own. I thought I was being empathetic and showing understanding and compassion by relating their story back to me, but what the universe was actually showing me was that I had a desperate need to listen to myself. This constant interruption and turning the spotlight back to myself was a mechanism I used for years. Finally, I was starting to understand it was an opportunity for me to open my eyes and ears to my inner self. The way I responded to others was not with empathy – it was with control. And my control showed itself most poetically via my interactions with my warrior child, Millie. After years of teenage turmoil, screaming matches over the breakfast table and endless retorts from Millie (that usually ended with, "You're not listening to me") I finally started to hear the message that life needed me to hear. Whenever I think of my children and the lessons they bring to me, I'm always reminded of this truly stunning piece of wisdom from Kahlil Gibran in his book, *The Prophet.*

> *"Your children are not your children.*
> *They are the sons and daughters of life's longing for itself.*
> *They come through you but not from you,*
> *And though they are with you yet they belong not to you.*
> *You may give them your love but not your thoughts,*
> *For they have their own thoughts.*
> *You may house their bodies but not their souls,*
> *For their souls dwell in the house of to-morrow,*
> *which you cannot visit, not even in your dreams.*
> *You may strive to be like them, but seek not to make*

them like you.
For life goes not backwards nor tarries with yesterday.
You are the bows from which your children as living arrows are sent forth.
The archer sees the mark upon the path of the infinite, and he bends you with his might that his arrows may go swift and far.
Let your bending in the archer's hand be for gladness;
For even as He loves the arrow that flies, so he loves also the bow that is stable.

Martyn's fighting spirit was carried into Millie's teenage years. As she battled with me to be heard, I battled to control life through filtering out what she was actually saying to me. For years I simply wasn't capable of hearing or responding to her feelings. I wanted everything to be OK. I was tired of the struggle, we both were. Millie and I had travelled a long road together with our shared experience of grief , hers for her beloved daddy and mine for my beloved Tony, we had a profound understanding of each other's pain. We had worked through all the grief with years of therapy, but here we were with this dark cloud over us and stuck in a pattern of not being able to communicate, which was hurting us both. The bond of love between us ran so deep that when anything challenged it, we both felt intensely wounded. Just when I thought I was making progress and working through my issues, I would end up projecting my anger at Millie, screaming at her the minute I came through the door after yoga, when I should have been all blissed out. I would have a complete temper tantrum about something totally unimportant, such as the dishes not being washed, or her room not being tidy. I found myself back in my old ways of conditioning and that nagging voice inside persisted with feeding me lies about the house needing to be perfect before I could be loved. Our interactions were at times explosive, and we were both shocked by the fierceness of what came out of our mouths. I didn't recognise the woman who was losing her mind and screaming at her daughter, I just knew that I wanted it to stop. Millie was and always will be my first great love in life, but I could feel the thread between mother and child pulling apart, and I didn't want her to go into adulthood hating me.

"Every day we miss opportunities for making true connections because instead of listening and responding appropriately to our children, we respond only from our point of view and fail to make a connection to their experience." [32]

This pattern of fight vs control was also the pattern I had with Martyn and my mother. I realised life was trying to show me that it was *my* pattern not theirs. It was only ever about *me.*

And now it was time to take ownership of it. This happened in the most profound way when Millie asked if we could do family therapy, as the last few years had been particularly difficult between us and we were both feeling it. I wasn't convinced and believed it was Millie who needed therapy in order to address her behaviour towards me. This was on the premise that when she sorted out her anger and rage we would be able to get along better. So I firmly placed the responsibility onto her and denied what was really going on. I was not averse to having therapy, I just couldn't see it as my problem. And that denial was part of the issue. In his book, *The Divided Mind*, John Sarno explains that when an ongoing situation fails to improve it is often an indicator that the time is right to seek out psychotherapy. By this time, the individuals involved are so entrenched in a cycle of blame and recrimination that the core issues are deeply buried and intervention by a qualified therapist is needed to bring them to the surface.

"Many patients will deny the existence of rage, for example at a parent. Others are unable to feel sadness, anger, disappointment, abandonment, and so on." [33]

It was my failure to look deeply at my issues that was the problem, this had nothing to do with Millie. Through her behaviour, she was teaching me about the rage, anger and sadness I was holding onto. The path to finally seeing this was truly profound.

By late October 2015, I was actually feeling pretty good about myself. I'd detoxed at the juicing retreat and done nothing apart from resting by the pool and doing some gentle yoga, generally switching off from daily life. I needed to be on my own without the children, without anybody knowing my story, without anybody actually knowing me. This ability to just slip into my own mind and space for a while in peaceful anonymity was so long overdue. Most of the other ladies on the retreat were city high flyers who were stressed to the eyeballs and needed to detox from their boozy, privileged London lives. When we all met on the first evening to introduce ourselves, the overwhelming reaction from the group towards me was, "Why do you need to be here?" And it was a good question. I looked so chilled out and blissful that many of them wanted a piece of what I had. But the truth was, the health and peace I exuded was mainly on the surface, and I still needed to go deeper to heal the wounds of the past. I needed to go deeper to heal my wounds with Martyn and to mend my relationship with my daughter. I had done a mountain of yoga and spiritual practice to get to where I was, but I needed psychotherapy to go deeper. I categorically wouldn't be where I am today without the help of my amazing therapist Lynne, who took me by the scruff of the neck and hit me hard with the truth. It was Lynne who told me, "*Dee, you've done an amazing job to be where you are but you've had, what we call in the business, a spiritual bypass. You're not dealing head on with the deep rooted issues of why you are feeling this way."*

Lynne was right.

And the irony of it all was that I found Lynne through my spiritual work, when I stepped inside Destiny Rising again at the beginning of November. I went looking for guidance, something, anything that could help me rebuild my relationship with Millie, which by this stage was hanging on by a thread. As I browsed the bookshelves, one of the girls at the counter asked if she could help, and I told her about my struggle with my daughter. She listened to me with love and compassion, as I ranted on, and then she pulled out a number from her phone and said, "Give Lynne a call. She will help you". And that was the moment when my east and west crossed over and I finally found my path to healing.

"Collaborative communication is the ability to expand our minds by taking in others' points of view and seeing our own viewpoint reflected in their responses." [34]

In our first few therapy sessions, Lynne spoke to Millie and I together. She could sense the willingness to heal and the love we had for each other, but she could also see how my inability to hear Millie's feelings had left this vast vacuum between us. This inability to hear was actually my own inner child crying out to be heard. My inner world was showing itself in my beautiful daughter, and in my insistence at always being right. The projected rage I was experiencing in my interactions with Millie was an accumulation of my own inner anger that had generated over many years and been repressed from childhood. But it was also the yes/no attitude that was stifling the creative expression in me, and which was symptomatic of the fifth chakra being out of balance.

"Creativity in the fifth chakra is a consciously willed process. We are literally making our world at each and every moment through our actions, expression and communication." [35]

It wasn't just my inability to see beyond black and white, right and wrong, yes and no, but I soon realised it was the basic reward system I used for my children and myself. I became increasingly aware that I was rewarding good behaviour and punishing bad behaviour, just as my mother and her mother had done, as well as a generation of Irish mothers before that. And this was not how I wanted to raise my children or, just as importantly, these weren't the restrictions I wanted to give myself. If I wanted to live in a creative stream of consciousness I needed to expand my thinking, which was stuck in a framework of a logical yes/no approach, and view life differently. This is beautifully highlighted in Edward De

Bono's work on lateral thinking in his book *PO: Beyond Yes and No.*

"Logical yes/no thinking is based on judgement but PO thinking is based on movement. Both types of thinking are necessary."

I needed to stop insisting on being right and stop trying to give others the answers. I needed to listen to me.

After the initial joint sessions with Lynne, Millie continued to do the work on her own, and I got on with the job of polishing my spiritual mirror. Then, in the summer of 2016, I stepped inside Destiny Rising again to have a second soul reading with Mandy and what she told me blew my mind. I will go into the details later on in the book, but what's important now is how she finished the reading. She said to me, "Who's Martyn?" I explained he was Millie's dad who had passed away, and then she replied, "You need to do some talking therapy around Martyn."

In that moment, I knew it was now my turn to speak to Lynne.

I got home and contacted her straight away.

"Dee, I've been waiting for your call," she responded.

As we talked over the coming weeks, Lynne helped me piece together my childhood story and understand how connected life was, and how I was truly responsible for my interactions with Millie and the world I was creating around me. She told me to read all the psychotherapy books I have referenced in this book and, as I devoured their wisdom, I could see how they applied to my life and story. Each week she brought me back to how I was feeling, knowing that I would try to talk at length about what was going on without saying much about how I actually felt. She empathised and listened because she could see in me a piece of herself. And, with great understanding, she said, "Dee, I know that meeting you is just as important to me as it is for you meeting me."

Lynne truly understood the nature of human interaction and listened so intently to me, not just for me, but for herself too. She helped me listen to my inner child and, as we focused intently on my feelings, I was being prepared for the journey into the sixth chakra and the all-seeing eye. And I hope in some ways I helped her see what she needed to hear.

She also taught me how to *consciously listen.* To listen with open ears, and to not interrupt conversations, it's a lifelong skill that I'm getting better at each day, although I'm not sure my kids would agree with you at times. Listen to the words that come your way from your loved ones and friends, and from the little people in your life. Those 'terrible twos' tantrums might have more to do with you than you think.

An Address to Children[36]

I rejoice to see you before me to-day, happy youth of sunny and fortunate land.

Bear in mind that the wonderful things you learn in your schools are the work of many generations, produced by enthusiastic effort and infinite labour in every country of the world. All this is put into your hands as your inheritance in order that you may receive it, honour it, add to it, and one day faithfully hand it on to your children. Thus do we mortals achieve immortality in the permanent things which we create in common.

If you always keep that in mind you will find a meaning in life and work and acquire the right attitude towards other nations and ages.

Albert Einstein

Our children truly are our future. They are an extension of the past just as we are, and they carry the same tendencies as we do, as well as their own unique selves. Listening to our children and being compassionate to their voice can bring us into perfect balance, as we see and hear our own inherent behaviours through their actions. Our children bless us with the perfect mirror and provide the opportunity to heal when we open to the oneness and connectivity of life and see the truth.

14

Learning To See

"We don't see things as they are,
we see things as we are."

Anais Nin

By the end of the year I was beginning to see myself for the first time through the eyes of my son, Fionn. I had always known that my son was sent to guide me. I knew this from the moment I held him in my arms and felt the energy of pure love in his tiny little body. Fionn is a very special boy, with great vision and wisdom that extends way beyond his eight years here on earth. And it was through this wisdom that he taught me about my own. He showed me that my third eye was open to the wonders of the universe.

It is our vision that constantly creates the path for our future and liberates us from the past. This is the work of Ajna, the sixth chakra, whose purpose is to perceive and command our reality.

"As we enter the third eye we can see where we have been, where we are now, and predict where we are going."[37]

The third eye is the energy centre of our inner perception. It is the screen where we project our desires and learn about them through images, archetypes and fantasies. As we open the third eye, we begin to bring conscious awareness to these desires, and the light of reality to all that is within us. We start to recognise how the patterns that have occurred in our lives have been sent to teach us something fundamental about ourselves, and we have those 'aha' moments where everything seems to suddenly make sense. Jung's process of individuation continues into the sixth chakra when we start to integrate and recognise the archetypal energies that affect our behaviour. In her amazing work on the chakra system, Anodea Judith correlates each chakra to Jung's archetype.

The Root Chakra is the Earth Mother/Provider
The Sacral Chakra is the Lover
The Solar Plexus Chakra is the Hero
The Heart Chakra is the Healer
The Throat Chakra is the Artist
The Third Eye is the Seer
The Crown Chakra is the Sage/Master

When we enter the sixth chakra, we start to see the bigger picture. We start to see the world from many different perspectives as we integrate the energies of these seven inner guides to give us wisdom and wholeness. We learn to call upon their guidance in different situations and recognise their differing viewpoints. For example, the lover in you will see something very different to the artist in you. The artist may well approach a situation with a critical eye, whereas the lover may see it from a more accepting place. When we learn about the archetypes we learn about our true nature. We start to see where we identify heavily with one and less so with another, and we are able to examine how this has impacted our lives through the patterns that have occurred in the past. This awareness gives us the freedom to break these patterns and create new behaviour. Archetypal energy manifests in what Jung called complexes, or the things we do or think, even though we may know better. So, for me this is that drink that takes me over the edge and makes me feel miserable the next day, or the critical voice that says, "You can't" when I know I can, or the doubt that filters in when I'm tired and feeling lonely. Also, we can embrace more than one archetype at any given time, which may cause conflict inside as different ones fight to be heard. When I'm battling with myself, I know it's often the archetypes at play. The artist in me may be crying out for solitude to write, whereas the lover wants to go out to play. Over the years, I have learnt the importance of honouring both, because if we punish and chastise the voice of an archetype we send it into the shadow realm where it will manifest into our lives through behaviors that we project onto others.

It was through the conversations I've had with my angel child, Fionn, that the strength of my own knowing was revealed to me. Fionn's faith is unfathomable. He just gets it, because the boy was born knowing. You can feel his presence when he walks into a room – he literally lights up the place. And he has a magical way with people where he is compassionate but fair. I have never met anybody else who I trust as completely as I do Fionn. I trust his wisdom, guidance, honesty, pureness and his truth. He is a reflection of my inner wisdom, but he's also just a little eight-year-old boy who wants to play and have fun.

One blustery November morning, Fionn and I went out to walk our little dog Yogi. The force of the wind was whipping at our sides as it carried us along the path into my magical woods. I had been curious about my son since his birth simply because I could sense something very calming about his nature. Most people feel it when they first come into contact with him. Millie is an atheist and feels my belief system about the connectivity and oneness of life is complete poppycock, but I was curious to see if any of my faith had filtered down to my son. It was something that had been circling around for a while, so I decided to ask him about it outright. My heart was to melt as I had the first of many conversations with my angel.

As we walked into the woods hand in hand, I stopped, bent down and looked into the massive brown orbs of his soul.

"Fionn, darling," I said, "Do you talk to angels?"

My son's response was proud and immediate.

"Yes, I talk to Angel Gabriel in my heart," he replied. "I talk to him when I'm stuck and he shows me the way with his light. He tells me to stay calm. He has light shining off his face. What angels do you talk to, Mum?"

My face lit up as I replied, "Oh…I talk to Gabriel, he's my favourite. I also talk to the main man, Archangel Michael."

And that was that, Fionn was on a roll. He spent the next 30 minutes having a conversation about the angels, the chakra system, crystals, telepathy, meditation and the meaning of life. I was blown away by what he just seemed to know intuitively. As we carried on chatting and little Yogi ran around our ankles, I realised life was showing me the meaning of gratitude and the great blessing of meeting Tony. There would be no Fionn without him. My beloved husband had given me the gift of love, which our little eight-year-old boy still carried in his heart.

As Fionn turned away to get on with the job of being a busy little boy, he said, "Daddy told me not to worry about him. I'm happy that he is in my heart. I know he's in your heart too, Mummy, because he loves you. I can tell."

As he skipped off into the woods to play with his dog I clutched my heart, looked up to the heavens and cried, "Thank you, thank you, thank you for the wonderful gift of my son."

And it was this love that gave me the strength to seek an alternative life outside the system. I was at a place in my life where I wanted something different for us both. Millie was approaching 18 and her path was set for completing her A Levels and going off to university to study film and history. She had grown into a strong, independent woman. The past had sealed that fate for her and I knew she was primed for a bright future in England living the life she wanted. But I wanted something different for Fionn and myself. It was now time to turn my attention to what was right for us. And something deep inside me knew that whatever it was, it wasn't in the UK…that something was my intuition.

"Intuition is the unconscious recognition of patterns. It is one of the four functions of Jungian typology – the others being sensation and feeling, related to the first two chakras, and thinking, which relates to chakra seven." [38]

Intuition is that little flicker in the belly, or that flutter of the heart, or that 'just knowing' – as I call it – when you feel beyond what is there with a level of certainty that is unexplainable. When we develop our intuition, we develop our psychic skills and our ability to see through the conscious surrender to the unconscious mind. This requires a huge amount of trust and practice as we learn to unscramble the messages that come to us. And, as with anything that requires practice, you don't always get it right! When we move into the higher realms of the sixth and seventh chakra we move beyond the realm of the individual self into a higher place of understanding and the collective consciousness.

"Insight
untangles the threadlike journey
of the self-seeking mind
and redirects its attention towards
unborn awareness."

Mooji

13th November 2015 was a day that will forever remain in my consciousness as the day of two halves. It was the day the world witnessed Paris' pain as she was brought to her knees by a violence and terror that made no sense. And it was also the day I met Magic Marina.

I met Marina through my beautiful soul sister, Alex, who, like me, is living her truth by helping others on the path to live theirs. Marina is an inspired psychic and I learnt more about myself in the two hours I spent in her presence than I've learnt in a lifetime. Marina came into my life when I was at a crossroads. Her ability to see the path ahead gave me the courage to make the change in my life that has brought me to where I am today. Through her inspired tarot reading, she brought into words the things that I knew in my heart, and she gave me faith and confidence to be me. I will always be truly grateful for her loving guidance and her brutal honesty! She told me my house in St Albans had a special energy and was a healing space, which is why I couldn't sell it. The house needed to stay because it was built out of love and would be a place where I might run workshops in the future, a place where others could learn. It was also a secure place for my son. She told me I was telepathic and that I can travel in space and time, which was true. I had played with past life regression in previous meditations and had travelled in time to a place where I walked in the woods as a young medicine woman, and as an old sage in Babylon. She also told me that I was clairvoyant, and that the cleaner my body becomes from alcohol, food and negativity, the more intuitive I will become. This was also happening to me on a daily basis – I was beginning to see the path ahead. Marina also said my life's purpose was to bring love and light to the world as part of a movement of global consciousness that was happening right now. That people could see how beautiful I was, but I could only see everyone as one. And this summed me up completely. Marina pretty much told me everything I already knew. I have this profound sense of duty and want to be the best I can be in this world, and this passion is bound by my understanding that everything is connected. She told me this book would be a success and I'd travel with it to America and beyond. She also informed me I had a connection with Louise Hay. I smiled when she said this, as I knew it was coming. Louise is the mothership…she is my hero. Louise's little book *You Can Heal Your Life* was the first self-help book I ever bought, back when I lived in Hong Kong. I was 21 and I've kept that precious copy and her magical words close to my heart ever since. She also told me I was getting younger, and that I was going to live to a very old age. Now this I really liked! I didn't just like it from a vanity point of view, but I actually felt myself getting younger as the weight of the past started to lift from my shoulders.

As Marina finished her reading, she asked, "Who's David?"

"I don't know anyone with that name," I replied.

"Well, look out for someone with that name," Marina instructed.

And so I did…and if only you could have seen the smile on my face when I met him a month later in India and said to myself, "Wow, that Marina really is magic!"

And so with Marina's encouragement and words ringing in my ears, I began to visualise a new way of being for Fionn and myself. And as I did I planted the seeds to a new life. I knew I wanted to raise him in a more sensitive environment where children played outside in nature and didn't wither away indoors on their electronics frying their brains and killing their imagination. I wanted him to be schooled somewhere where they valued his individuality as much as they valued their league tables. I wanted him to live somewhere that protected his sensitive nature and said it was OK to be different. Most of all, I wanted him to be somewhere that had a magical energy that fed his soul. Personally, I wanted to be somewhere that nourished my soul and healed my wounds. I wanted to leave the story behind and make a fresh start somewhere new with like-minded people. And I wanted to find love. Something very primal inside kept telling me that my man was not in the UK – he was somewhere else. And so I set my heart on this new way of being. I visualised and prayed, and then I set it free. I gave my trust to the universe and waited.

"Sixth chakra development is usually referred to as spiritual awakening. We suddenly see with new eyes, experience profound insight, change our perspective and attitude, or receive a vision. It can happen any time in life, but like the light of most dawns, it is often preceded by darkness." [39]

And I was awakening. I was doing the work and awakening the woman inside who had been silenced for years. I was seeing with new eyes, hearing with new ears, and feeling again with a heart that was open. I had walked through the darkness of the soul, the darkness of grief and loss, of longing and anger and betrayal to find this new woman staring back at me in the mirror. And now it was time for her to step into the light.

15

Leaving The Past Behind

"Darkness cannot drive out darkness; only light can do that. Hate cannot drive out hate; only love can do that."

Dr Martin Luther King, Jr.

On that same evening on 13th November 2015, I looked at my Facebook feed and cried as the world watched the horrors in Paris unfold as the heart was ripped out of the city of love in an atrocious attack on humanity that claimed the lives of 130 people and shone a spotlight on how divisive our world has become. And in that moment I was called to action. I had stood by and watched so much suffering and conflict in the world, especially over the past five years. The depth of grief in my personal life was mine alone, but it was also a reflection of the depth of grief on our planet as our beautiful world cried out in pain from the destruction caused by us all. I was feeling the pain and suffering from Mother Earth through my own experience, and there was no denying this suffering. The evidence was so clear that even a blind man could see the truth. As a global community of 7.5 billion people, we seem to be hell bent on killing our planet and killing ourselves. Recent reports from NASA's Global Climate Change: Vital Signs of the Planet website, the United Nations and the Institute for Economics and Peace show alarming facts, which include:

2015 was the world's hottest year on record. Global warming is fact.

The continent of Antarctica has been losing 134 gigatons of ice per year since 2002 – the Arctic Ocean is expected to become ice free in the summer by 2050.

More than one million species face potential extinction as a result of disappearing habitats, changing ecosystems and acidifying oceans.

There is a 90 per cent probability that human-produced greenhouse gases such as carbon dioxide, methane and nitrous oxide have caused much of the observed increase in the earth's temperatures over the past 50 years.

In 2012 to 2014, 805 million people were estimated to be chronically undernourished, according to the website of the Food and Agriculture Organization of the United Nations.

Since the turn of the millennium, the number of deaths due to terrorist activities has increased fivefold. This also coincides with US military campaigns in Afghanistan and Iraq, according to the website of the Institute of Economics and Peace.

I felt a deep sense of duty after the atrocities in Paris, on the night of November 13th 2015, which profoundly affected me as I tried to make sense of it all, and explain it to my children who were scared of the world we were living in. Millie had been out at a nightclub in London at the time of the Paris bombings. When she arrived home at 4am she fell into my arms like a small child. It seemed like the Paris attackers had achieved their goal because my beautiful, darling Millie was terrified. She had been dancing the night away at Café de Paris, a French nightclub in Central London, when the news of the attacks flashed up on the social media feeds that every young person seems to be addicted to these days. She watched, surrounded by the young French living in London, as they fell to their knees with grief, as they saw what was happening in their homeland. One moment they were dancing and having fun, the next they were on their knees crying. The pendulum of life had swung from joy to sorrow in that one split second. It is within these defining moments that transformation occurs. As Millie left the nightclub to make her way home, the city of London went into lockdown. The ripples of fear started to feed its way around the major capital cities of the world and they were put into a state of heightened security, in case further copycat acts were planned. The London Underground and bus services were pulled out of operation and Millie had to jump in a taxi to get herself back home to Hertfordshire. As I wrapped her in my arms to comfort her, I was reminded of the pain she felt when I told her the news of her father's death. It was as if that wound had been reopened and , as she drifted off to sleep, I knew I had to do something to ease the suffering .

It's difficult not to get consumed by the news at a time of tragedy when the horrors of terrorism monopolise every media outlet. I made a conscious decision to stop actively participating in the 'news' about three years ago, when I made a choice not to feed the fear and negativity that our news channels spew out on a daily basis. It doesn't mean I'm not compassionate and detached from world events, because I am still aware. I am more aware than most, but my awareness comes from a place of love. I do not need to be fed the news second-hand with someone else's agenda all over it to feel what is going on in the world. I can attune myself to its energy through the world that I feel in me, and bring light and love when there is darkness. This is my purpose in life. This is how I am actively participating in the movement of global consciousness that is shining a light on the world at a time of darkness. This book is my message to the world that says there is another way. If we imagine living in peace then we will live in peace, as the great John Lennon once said. If we do not give these people a platform to voice their hatred, then there is no platform to voice hatred. The news is about shocking the world, and the actions of these terrorists feed that shock.

"The Truth is one, but the Paths are many."

The Upanishads

The next morning, Millie was glued to the social media feeds that were consumed with the events of the previous night in Paris. It was hard to avoid, and I struggled to understand any of it. I couldn't comprehend how people could kill in the name of religion. You can't put religion in a box, or own some part of it, because religion at its heart is based on love. Our free will gives us the right to express that love in many ways, but there is still ultimately only one God – and that is love. And the truth is we are all searching for peace and happiness. We may find our way to it by being a Christian, a Hindu, a Muslim, a Buddhist or a Pagan, or by just following our hearts. Hinduism is at its very core a religion of unity and inclusion. The Hindu scriptures teach us 'vasudhaiva kutumbakam' – that 'the world is one family', which is the very essence of my belief. I believe we are one family bound by one consciousness. We are all branches on the tree of life.

"The Truth is there for us all to see. The sun does not disappear behind a cloud simply because a Christian or Muslim stands under it. The Gita shows us the way to live with God,

to live with each other and to live with
Mother Earth in peace and harmony." [40]

Love is beyond boundaries; it cannot be contained and it is constantly expanding and growing. No act of war, violence or injustice is ever done in the name of religion, because religion is rooted in love. These terrorists are not acting out of love, they are acting out of fear. And fear is energy, which can be changed.

"Everything is energy and that's all there is to it. Match the
frequency of the reality you want and you cannot help
but get that reality. It can be no other way.
This is not philosophy. This is physics"

Albert Einstein

In the ground-breaking book Power vs Force[41] by David Hawkins, the author shows how feelings vibrate energetically along a spectrum of consciousness, with the feelings of shame right at the bottom at 20KHZ and the feelings of enlightenment, which is ultimate consciousness, at the top at 700+ KHZ. When we force life we are operating at lower energetic levels of consciousness, and living in a world of shame, guilt, apathy, fear, desire, anger and pride. But as we know from the basic laws of physics, force always creates a counterforce. When we step into the full power of life, we operate from higher energetic levels of consciousness and live in a world of courage, neutrality, willingness, acceptance, reason, love, joy, peace and enlightenment. Force can only exist if it is pushing against something – it cannot exist as a wholeness on its own, which is why the opposite of force, i.e. power, *will always win the day*. So, when we respond to tragic events in the news with fear, we may think we are being compassionate, but we are actually colluding with it, because fear is low energy force. The only way to transcend fear is to act from higher levels of consciousness. I knew all about this through my own life, as I had sat in the depths of grief for so long. I have been there at rock bottom, at the lowest end of the energy spectrum, and I have pulled myself up and out of the other side. And the other side is where I walk hand in hand in my power of consciousness. I did this through my yoga practice, my meditation and through all the activities that I have described so far in this book. I lifted myself up from grief through the wounds of life that were controlled by fear and moved into the power of love, where I now live as a high energy being. And as I walk in the power of love I am healing others just by being me. Because those of us who walk in the light change the vibrations of those who don't. And that, my friend, is not hippie dippy shit – that is physics.

We can change our reality, and our life, by changing our frequency. Everything we do in life has either a positive or a negative energy, and this is held together by the life source of true love. Unfortunately, the judgements we make about ourselves limit positivity, which impacts our reality. This is why we feel amazing when we are in the presence of 'special' people like the Dalai Lama, Indian gurus or Tibetan nuns. It's because they are high vibrational people. The hours of meditation and service to God have helped raise their vibration to the highest levels of love, joy and enlightenment. I experienced this when I met H.H. Pujya Swami Chidanand Saraswatiji in 2018, and the feeling of just being in his presence was so blissful that I actually cried tears of joy. It felt as if I had met God himself. Just being close to him had a profound effect on my own energy field for days. To be loved, like the guru, is to be of service to the world and humanity. When we give more of ourselves to others, through service to the divine, we feed our hearts with love, and this love always comes back to us threefold.

My friend Finola and her daughter Ashley popped over that morning to have a catch up. They were late because they had been so engrossed in the news, and of course we all sat around and talked about the atrocities in Paris. I could feel the sadness and fear that it had created in our small world of five, and knew this fear must have been magnetised out to the world on a global scale. I didn't want to feed the hatred with any more fear and hatred, and I felt strongly that we needed to send Paris love. Millie looked at me in disbelief and came out with one of her classic one liners. *"Oh my God, Mum," she said, "you want me to hug a terrorist."* We all fell about laughing, and her comments broke the thickness of our suffering as our mood lifted immediately. I smiled to myself, as I could see that our energies had been raised, although I was mindful not to say anymore to Millie as I think she would have had me certified! But laughter does raise energy. Laughter vibrates at 540KHZ, which is high-level consciousness and explains why our world always feels so great when we have a good giggle. And yes, if I was honest I was in essence saying that we should hug a terrorist, maybe not physically, that wouldn't be advisable, but with compassion and empathy for their suffering. Because their suffering is also ours. Now that might be a hard thing to hear if you or a loved one have been a victim of terrorism or hatred, but it comes from a deep understanding that there is no other way. When the world is projecting fear and tragedy we must remember that there are seven billion *I*s, but only one '*we*'. When my children were fearful because of what had happened in Paris, I wanted them to know that this is a beautiful, loving world, and if they just believe it, they will see it, and if they see it, they will make it so, and their world will become beautiful and loving. To make the world a place of love we need to shine our love, even when our hearts bleed. And it starts with me. It starts with you. It starts with Maureen next door and Dave down the road and each and every one of us until the collective power to say no to hatred is squashed by the one and only true power – the power to say yes to love.

And to prove this point, I think the most defining news moment of the whole Paris coverage was when a lone pianist pulled up outside the Bataclan with his grand piano and played Imagine by John Lennon in the middle of a group of journalists. And in that moment this brave soul did more for world peace than any report from a major news outlet. He silenced the voice of fear and gave us the sound of love.

"As one of us awakens and rises,
it makes it easier for another to follow her lead.
RISE SISTER RISE."

Rebecca Campbell

As 2015 drew to a close, I started to get a deeper sense of just what those words meant. This happened through the spiritual sisterhood of my relationship with Jennifer, Alex and Taran. We all went through massive transformations in 2015, and we held the light up for each other to follow. I will talk more about this in the next few chapters, but all I will say now is that our lives were changed forever by our friendship. And I felt an inner peace within myself. The rewards of my spiritual practice showed on the outside, as my body felt light and expansive and a youthful glow replaced the grey sheen of grief that I had worn for so many years. 2015 was a transformational year where there was no going back and where I finally felt like I had the strength to leave the past behind. I found the courage to walk away from my old patterns of behaviour and learnt to balance the needs of the archetypal energies that presented themselves through me. I started to feel real compassion towards Millie and saw my relationship with her as an opportunity to heal the mother/child bond in me. I found the angel within me through the zen-like spirit of my son, who revealed more understanding of life than any book, teacher or person that I have ever known. That amazing little boy gave me hope that the evolution of mankind was moving forward, or should I say coming back to the truth which is unified in the oneness of our being. And I stood shoulder to shoulder with my new tribe in the sisterhood of consciousness that was rising up and lighting the way for the world to be a better place. And this light was guiding me back home, back to mother India, back to my heart and the final journey on my path to healing.

Winter 2015

It was in the beautiful icy stillness of winter that I came to the end of my search for a home. I'd found India again and my heart opened to the flow and showed me a new way of being. I spent a magical Christmas in the white sands of Agonda, South Goa, with my soul sisters, Jennifer and Alex, and experienced the freedom of living in the flow and letting go of control. India taught me how to be, and brought me into the seventh and final chakra on my journey of transformation. India taught me about non-attachment and opened me up to the universal identity of oneness. And India brought me love.

As I entered 2016, I stepped into a new space of consciousness, which taught me how to live from the heart. I became more aware about what was right and wrong for me through listening to my feelings and allowing my heart to guide me. When we live from the heart, the choices we make seem to be divinely orchestrated. And my heart told me that I needed to live in India. And so, with a renewed sense of purpose, I set about making the plans to move to India with Fionn. At times it was scary and I questioned what on earth I was doing, and at times when I sat in the quiet and contemplated everything that had happened to me in the previous year, it just seemed to make perfect sense. I knew I needed to let Tony go once and for all, and I knew that was intrinsically tied up in me finding myself and finishing my book. And, for some reason, I knew the magic would happen in India and the words would fly to me like they've never flown before. I could just sense it. But in the face of the greatest change comes the greatest resistance and I faced lots of it from my family, especially Millie, who thought I had finally lost the plot. But with my strengthened will through the work of the lower chakras, I had the fight in me to face this demon of attachment. And from this new height of being I could also see that this resistance wasn't theirs, it was mine. It was my ego at play. It was the frightened child that struggled to release the past. The battles I had with others were a reflection of my own inner battle to let Tony go. But I sat with it all with a renewed sense of knowing that I was doing the right thing.

Winter is a time for inner reflection, where the world stills itself, animals hibernate and the soul faces the cold and hard realities of life. We walk through a period of darkness as the days shorten, and we sit with the things that make us feel uncomfortable. But it is also the time when we finally break free from the cycles that hold us back. Doing this work is not easy, but doing it ultimately leads us to liberation. And the path is shown to us in the fourth noble truth of Buddhism, which is that freedom from suffering is possible by practising the eight-fold path. This path has the qualities of wisdom, meditation and morality. By the end of the winter I took my first step on this path, and it showed me the following key pieces of wisdom:

- ***To be in the flow you need to let go of control***. And I knew this. I knew this deep in my heart. The times I allowed divine universal wisdom to guide me and let go of outlining, second-guessing and pushing against life, were the times when the magic happened. This happened without fail every single time.
- ***The path of wisdom, meditation and morality was the way***. This is essentially about looking, seeing and being in the world from a place of love. It involves everything we do, from how we eat, to how we speak, to how we make money. We feed these through our meditation practice as we gain wisdom to be the best we can be in this world. And there is no end. We keep on moving, growing and expanding.
- ***To stay faithful to the heart, even in the difficult times.*** The heart never fails you. Even when you are

on your knees in the depths of despair, your heart will find a way to heal you. Your beautiful heart is your gift from God.

- ***We need to walk through the darkness to see the light.*** When we are in tune with the world as one, we cycle through the seasons with an appreciation that there will be dark times. But once we learn this great truth, it no longer hurts. We are no longer attached to the fact that there is suffering in life. And thus we return to the first noble truth that life is suffering. And we come full circle.

16

I'm Coming Home

"She had the soul of a gipsy,
the heart of a hippie
and the spirit of a fairy."

(Anonymous)

I booked to go to Goa for Christmas back in August 2015, not long after I returned from Thailand, where the seed was planted for another way of living and my desire to spend more time in South Asia was strong. I had been longing to go back to India for years, but the children were less than keen, to say the least. Millie had heard my stories of India countless times over the years as she grew up, and she knew from the passion in my voice that it held a special place in my heart. Now that she was approaching 18, she wanted to save up to go to India by herself. She wanted the backpacking experience. I understood this completely. Millie no longer wanted to be tied to her mother's coat tails and I didn't wish to keep her there. I needed to give her wings to fly. She wanted to experience India as a young, independent woman, just as I had, and there were very few countries left for her to see on her own, as I had pretty much covered all the big backpacker trails while taking her on my own travels. My passion for travelling never stopped when we had children, and Tony had the same passion, so for years Millie experienced many exotic holidays and tasted the pleasure of travel, not as a backpacker but in a five-star kind of way. And understandably, India was a bit of a hot potato with her. But I knew I needed to go and bargained with her that Goa wasn't really proper India anyway, and she still had the rest of her life to discover the vast subcontinent on her own. In fact, I think you need an entire lifetime to do India real justice, as it is a land of strikingly diverse cultures, landscapes, history and people. From the lush hill stations and Buddhist enclaves of the Himalayas to the Mughal glamour and jewelled cities of Rajasthan, to the tranquil charms of the Keralan backwaters. There's so much to see and do it's a never-ending discovery. And then there is Goa. Goa is a little oasis of calm all on its own, and the South, which is where I had my heart set on living, is still largely unspoilt and is as close to paradise as it gets. For 450 years Goa was a Portuguese colony. Then, in 1961, India reclaimed her. Her culture is an interesting amalgamation of both Eastern and Western styles, where Christians live peacefully alongside Hindus and Muslims. Christmas is celebrated as well as Diwali – the Indian festival of light, and restaurants serve Goan fish curry, which is influenced by Portuguese cuisine. In addition, her beautiful houses, which have wraparound verandas, are painted brightly as a mark of respect for the church, which is always white. Goa is the perfect mix of sun, sea, sand and spirituality – there's nowhere in India quite like it, which is why she's been home to travellers and hippies since the 1960s. The State of Goa is a state of two halves and attracts an eclectic mishmash of folk. In the north there's the backpacker and package holidaymakers who want to party to the best DJs in the world and visit the famous flea markets in Anjuna, sampling India for the first time in a semi-commercialised way. And in the South there's the hippie and First Marigold Hotel retirement crowd, who fell in love with India back in the day and want to recreate the magic and escape the cold winters of Europe in the unspoilt fishing villages that still feel authentically Goan. There is a magical energy in the sand that pulls you in and entices people back year after year. The waters of the ocean seem to cleanse your soul, and the minerals in the red earth connect you more deeply to Mother Nature. I feel more connected to source energy in Goa than in any another place in the world, and it is this connection that helps bring your dreams and visions to life. The other places that have a similar energy are Ibiza in Spain and Brighton in the UK. Along with Goa, these three places make up what I call the Golden Triangle of Light. And the new conscious movement of souls who are out there lighting up the way to make the world a better place seem to navigate around these three magical places. They are like the Holy Trinity of Light on earth. You feel the light when you visit, and if you don't then the place will not make it easy for your stay. I always tell people to be very careful what they wish for when they come to Goa, because they'll be standing on one of the world's greatest magnets. The charge from the minerals in the soil seems to magnetise your thoughts and whatever you dream about in Goa almost always comes true, 10 times faster than elsewhere in the world. This makes it a special place to head to and, as a result, Southern Goa attracts a beautiful community of healers, yogis and people who work in alternative therapies and pitch up for the season each year to share their gifts with each other and the world. It's one hell of a community, and to a large extent it's one led by empowered women. Those who sought to raise their children outside the system and in nature, away from the polluting mind of capitalism. Women who for so many reasons are on their own, by choice or by circumstance. Women who were open to the flow and welcoming to outsiders like me. And women who had great vision for the future. And something deep inside me knew I needed to be there so that I could grow into one of these women whom I'd admired from afar. I also knew I needed to be there to heal. And I always knew I would go back one day with Millie. I remember saying to her when she was a little girl that by the time she was 18 I would have taken her to India. I needed to honour my passage to India as she journeyed from childhood to adulthood. It was a way of honouring my need to go back to the mother. And so, rather reluctantly, Millie agreed to go to Goa, with the proviso that she could be home for New Year's Eve to party with her friends. And Fionn agreed to go as long as he wasn't dragged around the country. He just wanted to pitch up on a beach and do nothing. All I wanted was to go back to my beloved Goa. Not to Anjuna, where I'd spent time in my early twenties, but to somewhere quieter. Alex recommended Agonda beach in South Goa because she had been there a few times before and knew I would love the chilled vibe and the older, hippy crowd who had been around back in the day, just like me, and were now a bit more mellow and more into yoga and healthy living than hardcore partying. I knew it was the perfect place for me to be, but I wasn't up for being all bohemian and staying in a shack on the beach. I'm a rather shameless middle-class hippy these days who likes to stay in the coolest of hotels with all the benefits of air-con, fabulous décor and a flushing throne! I've done my time staying in bamboo huts, and I wanted a bit of luxury and barefoot sophistication, so I booked us in to H2O, which is the coolest pad on the beach. It was Christmas after all. Going to Goa turned out to be the best decision of my life. And to add to the deal, my two fabulous soul sisters, Jennifer and Alex, decided to come along for the ride with their families. And so Christmas in India was all set to be the most magical of affairs.

I flew out with Jennifer and the kids on 18th December, while Alex, her partner, Dan, and their three kids travelled there a few weeks earlier to make a longer holiday of it. I was excited to be going back to Goa. It had been a long time coming, but I felt nervous as there was a lot riding on India. She held my heart from years earlier when I was young and carefree, but what if I hated her now? What if I stepped off that airplane and the magic had gone? What if I no longer had that sense of adventure and freedom in my soul that I had in my twenties? What if that had been replaced by a tiredness of life and I could no longer appreciate the magic? You see, Goa was as much a test of the soul as it was of the senses. What if I no longer found joy in the colours and smells and in the vibrancy and madness that had taken my heart all those years ago? I'm not sure my heart could have coped with such disappointment, but I needn't have worried, because nothing had changed. The moment I stepped off the plane I could feel the magic inside. I could feel my soul. I could feel this longing deep inside that had been missing for so long. And I knew mother India did this to me. In fact, this time round, 25 years on, she felt even more magical, more life changing, more like home than ever before.

But first we had to deal with long queues in immigration and endless paperwork, which had "Welcome to India" written all over it. Anyone who has been to India will understand what I'm saying here! India has her own way of doing things. That's what I love about this crazy country, she will do things just as she pleases, and that's where the magic lies. It might not make sense to us, it might seem mind-bogglingly crazy and inefficient, but it's what she's doing anyway, and I loved that gentle confidence. The people carry this attitude with them too and however critical one might be of the system in India, the people have megawatt smiles and hearts that were open. I have always been blessed with the most amazing acts of kindness when I've been in India. The people with the least have given me the most, and I found this generosity to be truly humbling.

We made our way through customs in the record time of two hours, and drove 90 minutes through the early evening dusk to our fabulous hotel on Agonda beach. Then we said hello to paradise. Home for the next 10 days came in the shape of a fabulous boutique-style hut right on the beach with its own veranda overlooking the ocean, a dressing area suitable for my teenage fashionista and a stunning outdoor bathroom. The restaurant spilled out onto the beach, where you could sit on a daybed while watching the sun go down, and even though it was Christmas and peak season, it was pleasantly quiet. The vibe was calm and laid back, just how I liked it.

We soon got into our groove and settled into the chilled Agondan vibe. We spent our days lazing on the beach and mooching along the main street to buy knickknacks from the local traders, haggling over 10 rupees and getting into the Indian way of bartering for everything. By night we enjoyed the delicious Goan cuisine in one of the beach shacks as we watched the sun go down and the sky dance in shades of pink and orange, marvelling at the spectacular show from Mother Nature. This was my kind of Christmas. I was on an amazing beach with my beautiful children, my two soul sisters and their families, and I didn't have a care in the world. I could taste the freedom. I felt like my search was over. I can't quite explain it, but I just felt happy to be. I felt aligned to my inner self, as my heart opened and the magical sands of Agonda beach carried me back to my true self. And that self shone in Goa. Jennifer commented on it,

"Dee," she said, "I've never seen you come so alive. You look so light and beautiful."

It was true. I was alive in Goa. It was my special place. By the end of the holiday everyone was teasing me and calling me the Christmas fairy because I used to light up the place with my megawatts smile, just like the locals. And our collective mantra for the holiday was "I'll go with the flow". We didn't plan or organise anything in particular, we just went with what came in that moment and found ourselves wherever we were meant to be. We were at peace in the moment and ready to receive our blessings. Following years of struggle, I was beginning to see the simplicity of life when you stop controlling everything and start to allow life to just be. I really felt India was trying to teach me another way to live. She was teaching me to trust, and to be open to the world of possibilities beyond the limitation of my mind. She was teaching me a lesson in not having to try so hard. The girls could see the transformation in me. As they went off to yoga and tried to coax me along, I said I really didn't feel like I needed it. I was happy to stroll up and down the beach and be on my own. I didn't want any outer influences to feed me, I wanted to be guided by the healing properties of the sand and the sea. It was quite remarkable really considering I was an avid Yogi and practised five times a week, but once I opened my heart and listened to it, I couldn't deny what she wanted. I did, however, show up to one class. This was mainly because I'd promised Jennifer I would go with her one morning, and I always keep my promises. The teacher handed around a bowl with small pieces of folded paper that contained inspired words inside. We were invited to select a word and set our intention for our practice that day on whatever the word was. The words themselves were random, and I had no idea what I was picking up. So imagine my surprise when I unravelled my piece of paper to find the word 'control' written on it. I realised it wasn't random at all – it was divinely orchestrated. Of all the gazillions of words in the universe, I picked the one that was holding me down and keeping me blocked. Control. It was perfect. The universe was showing me I was meant to be in that yoga class on that morning in December in magical Goa. I was exactly where I was supposed to be. And this is how India taught me. She kept showing up to remind me that life only ever happens in the moment when we let go of control and start living in the now. I knew it. The card knew it. Life knew it. And my blessing for going with the flow was meeting David.

David showed up one afternoon right out of the blue, quite literally, in a holistic centre called The Space, which is situated outside Agonda beach on the Palolem Agonda Road in the most idyllic spot overlooking the jungle. I took a trip out there one afternoon with Jennifer, Alex, and the two boys – my son, Fionn and Alex's youngest son, Spike – to grab some food in the vegetarian café situated in an enchanted garden overlooking a field full of water buffalo. The Space is a haven for healers and therapists, who come from all over the world to hang out and run workshops and retreats. The maze of rooms, set in a beautiful old Portuguese mansion, are full of interesting trinkets and health foods to buy, and there is a large Yoga Shala in the jungle garden out the back. It's the perfect place to rejuvenate, meet like-minded people and eat great cakes! As the children played by the fountain in the garden on the front veranda, Jennifer and I wandered around the shop and read about the various therapies on the notice boards dotted around the place. I picked up a leaflet on myofascial release massage and as we poked around the various rooms in the back of the house, I noticed a rather handsome guy coming out of a room. We struck up a conversation with him and I asked if he knew about myofascial massage.

"Yes, I'm the therapist," he replied. "I'm David."

He talked about the benefits of the myofascial release technique and I was drawn in by his enthusiasm and gentleness. I had a niggling feeling there was something important about him. Later that evening, I spoke to Jennifer about it. Alex, Jennifer and Taran, my yoga teacher, are like my spiritual sages. They are my favourite people in the world to turn to whenever I need to discuss anything to do with my spiritual growth. I trust their wisdom implicitly and I know they are divinely aligned with me. They completely see me as I completely see them, and I know our paths have crossed for a reason. There is no denying this. We are all doing our thing to grow as souls in the knowledge that as we do so we are helping others along the way. We are and always will be bound by a sisterhood that wants to make the world a better place. When I told Jennifer that I thought there was something special about David, she smiled and said knowingly, "He couldn't take his eyes off you. There's definitely a connection there!"

I laughed at her and replied, "Don't be so stupid, he's gay. The good looking ones always are."

"I'm telling you, he's not and he liked you, Dee."

I think my lovely Jennifer was trying a spot of matchmaking! She knew my pain and loneliness and wanted me to find love as much as I did. As I laughed off her comments there was that little niggle of intuition inside that just wouldn't go away. There was something important about David. Then I remembered my reading with Magic Marina and her parting words to me, which were, "Who's David?"

And here I was in South Goa about to find out. I didn't tell the girls about Marina's vision, that would have sent them into overdrive, but I did book in for a massage a few days later so I could check David out a little more. The treatment was absolutely amazing, and David was pretty damn amazing too. He had a serenity and gentleness that belonged to someone who truly loved what they were doing, and I felt the healing powers from his touch. So, when I came back from my treatment all glowing and full of smiles, Jennifer was waiting and uttered a rather knowing, "Well?"

I just laughed at her again, but I could tell she had plans for me! And so David and I became friends. He was quite unlike any man I had ever met. He has a strong feminine energy, and is sensitive and compassionate to others. Not the usual red-blooded alpha type I seemed to attract. He cares deeply for the world around him and conducts his life in such a way that his happiness is his first priority. He spends half the year in Goa making money through massage and spends the rest of his time travelling around Europe and Asia. He sold his big house in London to finance his lifestyle, and is seemingly unattached to possessions or people, choosing to live with the freedom of coming and going as he pleases. He seems at genuine peace with himself and happy in his rather handsome and youthful skin, which belies his 50 years on earth. In some ways, I felt that David and others like him had paved the way for a lifestyle that appealed to the way I wanted to be. He seemed to appear out of the blue everywhere I went, and as I watched him from the outside, I started to ask myself what was so important about this guy. Was it his free spirit? His lifestyle? His energy? I couldn't quite put my finger on it, but I knew he was sent to teach me and that we would remain friends. And the morning before we were due to leave India, I had a moment of knowing. I sat the children down, looked at them both and said that I wanted to live in Goa because something deep inside was calling me to stay. It came from my inner self. Not from my plotting mind but from a deep sense of love in my heart, which ached for India to be home. And that's when I remembered the signs I received all throughout December when the Diddy song *Coming Home* played constantly in my head every morning and night. I'd shut my eyes and listen to the words. I couldn't escape that song – it was my soul singing to me because she knew she belonged to India. So in that moment I made the biggest decision of my life : to move to Goa. It was time to let life, love and God bring me what I needed. I opened my arms and embraced without question the guidance that said this was the path for me. The 46-year-old woman had nothing to do with it. I let go of control. And as I sat there cuddling the children with my newfound sense of freedom, I caught a glimpse of David swimming across the ocean, looking so graceful as he glided through the waves. When it was time to leave Goa and head home to England, I remember collapsing on the floor of Mumbai Airport sobbing my heart out just as I had 25 years earlier as I looked up to Jennifer and said, "I don't want to leave, this is my home." And she comforted me as she always did and said knowingly, "You'll be back, darling, if anyone can make it happen, you can, Dee, you'll be back."

It was with a heavy heart that I arrived back in England and walked through my front door, feeling the sorrow and pain of the past all over again. I no longer wanted to be in my beautiful home. England became my holding space as I made plans to return to India and start my new life. Within three days I had sealed the deal. I booked our return for 22nd March 2016 – exactly one year on from the most transformational year of my life.

17

Living Beyond Limitation

"I bow down to your stinky muddy dog paws, oh great guru of unconditional love." [42]

Learning to keep on moving was the realm of the seventh and final chakra on my journey to healing the self. The crown chakra is called Sahasrara, which means thousandfold, and its purpose is to help expand and grow consciousness beyond the limitations of identifying with the individual self and to a place of universal identity. This is the ultimate purpose of our spiritual practice, where we see from the eyes of oneness and realise finally that everything is connected. And to get to this place we have to let go of attachment and follow the path of wisdom, meditation and morality. For me, attachment was just another word for control. And when we control we are not trusting the wisdom of the universe to give us what we need, we are actually pushing against our suffering rather than seeing it as our greatest teacher. And I fully appreciate that for anyone who has suffered this lesson it is a tough one to get a handle of.

"When we are sure we know something we run the risk of closing down the crown chakra. New information requires us to expand our belief system, and the refusal to do so closes our system." [43]

My seventh chakra was out of balance because I had got to a place where I was fixated on knowing all the answers to life. I started to develop a new level of certainty that stopped me being in the flow and put me right back to square one, as I tried to manipulate and control life again. I was convinced I had all the answers and I needed the assurance of being able to predict the future. 'Knowing' was my new buzzword, "I know........" this or that or whatever but Jennifer would always reply, "No, you don't, Dee, you don't know, nobody knows."

And she was right, because whenever I thought life was taking me in one direction, I usually ended up going in the other. Life had a plan for me that was far greater than I could ever imagine – and there really was no second-guessing it. The only way to find inner peace was to stop trying to control and manipulate my life, and to start letting it flow through me, allowing the plan to reveal itself minute by minute. I was going round in circles. I knew all this intellectually but living and being in the flow was not always easy, and I didn't always get it right.

And so I entered the realm of the seventh chakra with a lot of confusion about what to trust. I had evolved through my own suffering to get to a place where I was consciously listening to my inner voice, and I felt like I could trust my intuition. My heart had opened and I started to feel my feelings and use them to guide my decision-making process. But I still needed to see beyond my own limitations, which if I'm honest kept me attached to my desires. The hopeless romantic in me was still looking for its happy ever after, and much of my spiritual development was done in the name of finding a romantic partner. It seems almost juvenile to admit that now, but it's the truth. It was done for my better good and not the good of mankind. It was done to heal the wounds of the mother/child bond and not the bond of Mother Nature. And it was calculated. I travelled this path because I wanted to heal me. And the seventh chakra healing is beyond all of that. It takes you to a place of being where wants and desires are removed from the equation. It is only when we surrender everything that has kept us bound to a way of being that we truly benefit from the limitless abundance of being.

What does 'being' mean? It means letting go of the need to be right in favour of listening to others' opinions and finding the lessons in what they are telling you. It means examining our belief systems and questioning them. When we say things such as, "I am an artist and artists never make any real money," we are binding ourselves to this belief system and making it our truth. But the fact is it's not true. Personally, I have been stuck in a belief system that told me I wasn't good enough and that I was somehow damaged by my story. These are my beliefs and mine alone. I bind myself to them. Nobody else has that power over me. Nobody. Stepping into the realm of the crown chakra is about stepping into the higher self and the archetype of the witness, which is why meditation is so vital in developing the seventh chakra. When we witness life we allow ourselves to receive information, and when we receive information we are receiving our blessing and stepping into our God-given right to heal and find wholeness.

One of the books that has helped me step into the world of seventh chakra healing is *The Four Agreements* by Don Miguel Ruiz. The book shares four basic agreements to living a life of wisdom. These are:

Be impeccable with your word.
Don't take anything personally.
Don't make assumptions.
Always do your best.

Be impeccable with your word means you really need to think before opening your mouth, which for me is a practice of containment because I have so much to say and I'm not afraid to say it! I would actually benefit by remaining silent more often, allowing others to have a voice. But it also means be mindful of the words you use, the words that say, "I can't" or "I'm not there yet" or "if only I had more money" or "he's just not my type". Because all these words put limitations around us, and bind us to a negative belief system that blocks us from accessing the abundance of universal love that is available to all.

Don't take anything personally means taking responsibility for only the things you are responsible for. Your words belong to you and not to anybody else. And so the same applies when you are on the receiving end of words or actions that are hurtful or unpleasant. Those words cannot hurt you, they only hurt the voice that feeds them. So if your children are screaming at you, don't take it personally – that's their inner voice saying, "I'm hurting." Give them a big hug instead and watch their suffering melt away. That's not to say we invite bad behaviour into our life. We don't. But we know how to guard ourselves against it through nonattachment.

Don't make assumptions is about those times when we get ourselves into a right pickle by misinterpreting a situation. It's OK. We all do it. There is no second-guessing in life. If we want to live authentically we need to judge each moment on how we feel in that moment, rather than having preconceived ideas and judgements about how things are.

Always do your best means that when you are trying as much as you can you are standing up for yourself and saying, "I'm good enough." You are accepting yourself just as you are in that moment. When you do your best you step outside your limitations because there are no limitations if what you have done is your best. And when you do your best you give yourself permission to make mistakes and learn from them. Doing your best is not an excuse to stand back and be complacent, because that wouldn't be doing your best. It means giving yourself permission to love yourself moment by moment, because you approve of yourself for doing your best.

Once we awaken as a being of consciousness, our whole experience of our story and the world as we see it awakens and we start to experience our life in a very different way. This is how we get to change the story of the past and heal the wounds that continue to hurt us in the present. We start to bring this conscious stream of awareness back down through the chakra system. At the brow chakra, we start to shine light on the story and see the bigger picture, not just our part in it. At the throat chakra we start to bring inspired thought into our creativity rather than struggling to find its voice. The voice of creativity now has clarity and purpose. At the heart chakra, we see beyond our own needs and struggles in our relationships with ourselves and others and start to develop compassion. As we work through our own issues, we look on as the relationships around us improve as a result of the wisdom and compassion we are now showing ourselves. At the solar plexus chakra, we turn forced action into transformative action as we energise our intents with vision, wisdom and communication. At the sacral chakra, we make connections with others at a deeper soul level, and we experience love and sexuality at a deep tantric level. And finally, at the root chakra, we bring all the virtues of compassion, wisdom, light and inspiration into our physical reality as we create a world and a life worth living. And we come full circle.

A year after I started on this journey, on 22nd March 2016, I stepped on a plane to India to start a new life with Fionn. This was a life I could never have imagined had I not stopped pushing against mySelf and started to listen to the quiet voice within.

My little boy was welcomed into a new school called The River House Academy on the banks of the Talpona River in South Goa. The school was set up by an inspirational group of women who live and work in Goa and wanted to provide a learning environment which inspires children to become confident, passionate and active global citizens. I knew it was the right place for Fionn the minute I stepped foot through the door. As Fionn settled into school, I searched for somewhere for us to live. I found the perfect place – a 3-bedroom villa with air-conditioning and Wi-Fi. Everybody told me I'd never find anything like that in Agonda but I did find it, or rather it found me. And like every other magical moment that has happened to me since I stepped foot in Goa, they all seemed to find me at exactly the right time, when I needed them most. This is how *being* showed itself to me. I haven't had to search for anything – everything I have needed or wanted has come to me. It has been truly remarkable.

I also met up with David again, who appeared out of nowhere, as he always did , while I was mooching along the road one day. He was preparing to leave for Europe after a long season in India was planning to hit the festival scene and live on the road as he partied the summer away and allowed life to take him along in the flow. He was as soft, sensitive and connected as ever, but I released we would only ever be friends. He is not the man in my letter to the universe – that guy is yet to reveal himself. But David was the catalyst to bring me back to life in India, and for that I will always be truly grateful. I knew I wanted to meet someone like him – someone with the same conscious awareness and energy and someone who is on the same level as me – and something told me that my path to him was via India. David taught me a new way of being where there are no should haves, could haves and would haves. He truly lives moment-to-moment, accepting what life gives him. His seemingly ideal lifestyle is worlds apart from mine, but he taught me that freedom is not about a lifestyle. Freedom is about moment-to-moment living wherever we are in the world.

The season in South Goa comes to an end by the middle of May, as the temperatures rise and the rains come in. Most Westerners return to their homeland for the long, hot monsoon months, as restaurants and shops close down and the beaches and villages are returned to the locals. I returned to the UK for the summer, but the UK was not where I wanted to be. My beautiful house in St Albans – the house that was the little girl's dream – no longer felt like home. I was consciously aware of this feeling of being suspended in time. It was as if the four walls of the house held all the pain and suffering of my past, and I could feel myself being sucked back into the story and the life that I so desperately wanted to leave behind. My soul had moved on and although I tried to enjoy those summer months as best as I could, the truth was I couldn't wait until September to be back on Indian soil again. I was willing my life away and counting down the days until our return. But, in another cruel twist of fate, life stopped me in my tracks and pulled me right back into the story I so desperately wanted to leave behind.

On 10th August 2016, at 7.30am, I received a phone call from my friend, Emma. I listened to her sob her heart out in stunned silence as she told me the tragic news that her husband Ray Theobald – Tony's best friend – had died instantly of heart failure the night before. I could not believe what I was hearing. In the midst of her suffering she said to me, "Dee, you're the only person in the world who understands. My whole world has just ended." And this I did know. I knew all too well as the wounds of grief cast their spell on me once again and I mourned the loss of our beautiful Great Raymondo, as we used to call him.

Ray and Tony were inseparable best friends and were like an old married couple. They initially met at work, but their work friendship blossomed into a brotherhood. They called each other every day and spent weekends and holidays together indulging their passion for golf. Ray was also an unmistakable giant of a man who battled with his weight. In his prime he topped the scales at around 32 stone. And there was no hiding when you were in his company. People were drawn to his size but also to his larger than life character. And my children loved their great big bear that was uncle Raymondo.

When Tony died, Ray was absolutely heartbroken, and he set about making big changes in his life to get healthy in honour of his best friend. He lost half his body weight and went to the gym every day. To the outside world he looked like he had regained his fitness and his chance for a healthy life. He also found love in his beautiful wife Emma and the scene was set for their happy ever after when they married in February 2015. And just like it had with Tony, his life ended in the blink of an eye and without warning. And yet again the close group of old friends, were united once more in our shared grief for a life lost too young. This was a hard one to make sense of. And I cried for days. It hurt deeply, and again I felt the wounds of loss and love were as much for Tony as they were for Ray, as I was once again challenged to accept life as it was.

As I walked through pain and surrendered to the tears, I felt like my heart had shattered all over again. But about a week later, Tony's brother called me and said, "Dee, I have something to tell you. We were walking along the marina the day after Ray died and Mum spotted two yachts that were moored up for the day. One was called the Lady Dee and the other one was called the Lady Emma. What are the chances of that? Well, I've come to a place in my life where there are no chances. There are no coincidences. I can no longer accept that life is just a sequence of random events, and I sensed the universe was trying to tell me something. As I closed my eyes and listened to my heart, the message I received was very clear. I was being told that those two friends were reunited again in death. Whatever their connection was through their earthly lives, there was no denying that they were joined again together in spirit. Tony and Ray were still here, and I was being called to share this message with the world.

We said goodbye to the great Raymondo on 6th September 2016, and the next day Fionn and I left the UK and flew back to Goa. And of course, India had plans for us straight away. We didn't move to the dream house in Agonda, as I had intended. Instead we were guided to an area called Patnem, which was much closer to Fionn's school and closer to the community of mums who welcomed us in with open arms and helped us make the transitions to our new life so much easier. It was the right place to be. Fionn settled back into his Indian school and I went about transforming our two-bedroom apartment into a beautiful home for us both. As I did I took time out to reflect on the past year and all the amazing lessons that life had brought to me. I felt strength in myself and in the undeniable connection that shone brightest in the women I call my soul sisters: Alex, Taran and Jennifer. As the light within me started to grow, this divine feminine energy invited me to a place deep inside, where I started to experience the wholeness of what it means to be a woman. I encountered the goddess in her many manifestations, and I also experienced her darker side and her shadow. And, as we started to rise as a collective, our stories began to feel familiar, and the themes that played out in one life also played out in the collective consciousness of other women. I started to recognise that I had my story, but it was also bound to other women's stories. These were stories of love and loss, faith and betrayal and awakening and change. As I grew stronger and started to heal, so did they. The year 2016 became an irrefutable year of connectedness and transformation, not just for me, but also for my soul sisters, who made life-changing moves that set them on a path to a new way of being.

Alex and her family moved to Ibiza to be close to the nurturing energy of the island. She has a vision to one day run a centre to help people find an alternative way to heal cancer. Taran and her children moved to an idyllic farm in the Peak District, Derbyshire, where she opened Holy Cow Yoga, the first yoga studio in the area. And Jennifer and her children moved to Brighton, where she is developing her skills as a heart healing intuitive oracle card reader. Of course, there were times when we were frightened, or we questioned what the hell we were doing, but in those moments of doubt one of us was always on the end of the phone to support the other and offer encouragement. As we called upon the sacred feminine energy to rise, it gave us the power to be greater than we ever could have imagined. And as we healed the wounds of our pasts and incorporated this wisdom into our everyday lives, we learnt to receive the wisdom of the generations of women before us. We began to see the archetypal female energy of the lover, the healer, the priestess and the crone in ourselves and in each other, and we drew upon this power, love and wisdom to reinvent ourselves. We started to feel and experience the true oneness of life, through the consciousness that holds us in its heart

And after I completed decorating my new apartment, I set about finishing this book. I knew it would be the final piece in the jigsaw to opening my heart and letting Tony go. The book had been holding on as much as I had, and I wanted it to fly so I could get on with my life. But the path to healing is not a quick fix. I'm still the student finding her way, and as I settled into my life in Goa, I realised that my healing had only just begun and there was way more to come. India was healing and revealing parts of me that I never knew existed. And it turned out there was more than just one book that I need to let fly. Letting Tony go was one thing, but healing the wounds of my past had become a bit of a masterpiece. Suddenly I realised that I was writing three books, as part of a body of work on unity consciousness, which I have called *The Truth is Within*.

Unity consciousness means seeing the world through the eyes of oneness: acting and believing in the collective one, with nature, life itself, our own divine grace and with other people. It means seeing the world with new eyes, hearing it with new ears and loving it with a new heart.

The wisdom that I am receiving to write these amazing books that I feel I have been called to write, is weaving itself into my personal story moment by moment. The more I delved into my own heart and trusted the wisdom that came to me, the more beautiful, synchronistic events appeared out of nowhere and book two, which is called *The Truth – Is the Art of Being*, just sort of wrote itself. My second book is based on the teachings of *The Tibetan Book of the Dead* and *The Pagan Book of Living and Dying*. And soon it became very clear that through my own experiences of death, I was being taught the art of living.

As I started to think about sharing my work with the world, and getting my stories published, I ran into Cory Goldberg, an American photographer who has been living in India for over 10 years. I wanted to do a photoshoot for the cover of my books and I had an image in mind. I explained to Cory about my shamanic journeying, which I described earlier on in this book, and how in my vision I was always walking across a bridge to be met by someone amazing on the other side.

And one day, as I drove past Fionn's school and followed the road for about five minutes, I came across the most beautiful bridge that I have ever seen. It is called the Sadolxem footbridge. Suddenly I had found my bridge, the bridge I always visualised when I did my shamanic journeys. Cory took the photograph on the front cover of this book on that bridge on 12th November 2016. Cory understood me and could see my vision. I am truly grateful to him for the sublime images he produced; they captured the moment when my heart opened, and he gave me wings so that I could fly. These images were just one of the many blessings I went on to receive when I started living from the heart.

I soon learnt that the bridge I was crossing was not a physical place as such, but more a metaphor for the journey the soul takes as it moves from this world to the next. It is a journey we all take as our souls cross the sacred threshold to the other side. In the end it was Tony's love that led me there, to the life I am leading now in India. I would not be here if he hadn't died. His death breathed new life into mine, another gift from him that I simply could not have imagined before.

And so the journey continues…

CITATIONS

1. Tom, and Judi Sion. 2002. The Magdalen Manuscript: The Alchemies of Horus & the Sex Magic of Isis. London, UK: ORB Communications.
2. Saraswati, S. C. 2006. Drops of Nectar: Timeless Wisdom for Everyday Living. New Delhi: Wisdom Tree.
3. Saraswati, S. C. 2006. Drops of Nectar: Timeless Wisdom for Everyday Living. New Delhi: Wisdom Tree.
4. Saraswati, S. C. 2006. Drops of Nectar: Timeless Wisdom for Everyday Living. New Delhi: Wisdom Tree.
5. Saraswati, S. C. 2006. Drops of Nectar: Timeless Wisdom for Everyday Living. New Delhi: Wisdom Tree.
6. Peck, M, S. 2006. The Road Less Travelled. London, UK: Arrow.
7. Lewis, C. S. 1989. A Grief Observed. London, UK: Harper Collins.
8. Saraswati, S. C. 2006. Drops of Nectar: Timeless Wisdom for Everyday Living. New Delhi: Wisdom Tree.

9. Judith, Anodea. 1996. Eastern Body, Western Mind: Psychology and the Chakra System as a Path to the Self. Berkeley, CA: Celestial Arts.
10. Judith, Anodea. 1996. Eastern Body, Western Mind: Psychology and the Chakra System as a Path to the Self. Berkeley, CA: Celestial Arts.
11. I've chosen not to name him to protect his identity.
12. Judith, Anodea. 1996. Eastern Body, Western Mind: Psychology and the Chakra System as a Path to the Self. Berkeley, CA: Celestial Arts.
13. Norwood, Robin. 2008. Women Who Love Too Much. New York City, NY: Pocket Books.
14. Norwood, Robin. 2008. Women Who Love Too Much. New York: Pocket Books.
15. Storr, Anthony and C. G. Jung. 1983. The Essential Jung: Selected Writings Introduced by Anthony Storr. Princeton, NJ: Princeton University Press.
16. Rogers, C. R. 1967. On Becoming A Person: A therapist's view of psychotherapy. London, UK: Constable.
17. Scaravelli, Vanda. 1991. Awakening the Spine: The Stress–Free New Yoga that Works with the Body to Restore Health, Vitality and Energy. London, UK: Harper Collins.
18. Seifer, Nancy, and Vieweg, Martin. 2009. When the Soul Awakens. Reston, VA: Gathering Wave.

19. Vitale, Joe, and I. H. Len. 2007. Zero Limits: The Secret Hawaiian System for Wealth, Health, Peace, and More. Danvers, MA: John Wiley.
20. Judith, Anodea. 1996. Eastern Body, Western Mind: Psychology and the Chakra System as a Path to the Self. Berkeley, CA: Celestial Arts.
21. Storr, Anthony and C. G. Jung. 1983. The Essential Jung: Selected Writings Introduced by Anthony Storr. Princeton, NJ: Princeton University Press.
22. Waheed, Nayyirah. 2013. salt. Charleston: Createspace.
23. Waheed, Nayyirah. 2013. salt. Charleston: Createspace.
24. Steiner, Rudolph, and Michael Wilson. 1964. The Philosophy of Freedom. Forest Row, UK: Rudolf Steiner.
25. Judith, Anodea. 1996. Eastern Body, Western Mind: Psychology and the Chakra System as a Path to the Self. Berkeley, CA: Celestial Arts.
26. Peck, M, S. 2006. The Road Less Travelled. London, UK: Arrow.
27. Storr, Anthony and C. G. Jung. 1983. The Essential Jung: Selected Writings Introduced by Anthony Storr. Princeton, NJ: Princeton University Press.
28. Judith, Anodea. 1996. Eastern Body, Western Mind: Psychology and the Chakra System as a Path to the Self. Berkeley, CA: Celestial Arts.

29. Judith, Anodea. 1996. Eastern Body, Western Mind: Psychology and the Chakra System as a Path to the Self. Berkeley, CA: Celestial Arts.
30. Waheed, Nayyirah. 2013. salt. Charleston: Createspace.
31. Judith, Anodea. 1996. Eastern Body, Western Mind: Psychology and the Chakra System as a Path to the Self. Berkeley, CA: Celestial Arts.
32. Siegal, D. J. and Mary Hartzell. 2014 Parenting from the Inside Out: How a deeper self-understanding can help you raise children who thrive. Victoria, Australia: Scribe.
33. Sarno, J. E. 2006. The Divided Mind: The Epidemic of Mindbody Disorders. London, UK: Harper Collins.
34. Siegal, D. J. and Mary Hartzell. 2014 Parenting from the Inside Out: How a deeper self-understanding can help you raise children who thrive. Victoria, Australia: Scribe.
35. Judith, Anodea. 1996. Eastern Body, Western Mind: Psychology and the Chakra System as a Path to the Self. Berkeley, CA: Celestial Arts.
36. Einstein, Albert. 1935. The World As I See It. London, UK: John Lane.
37. Judith, Anodea. 1996. Eastern Body, Western Mind: Psychology and the Chakra System as a Path to the Self. Berkeley, CA: Celestial Arts.

38. Judith, Anodea. 1996. Eastern Body, Western Mind: Psychology and the Chakra System as a Path to the Self. Berkeley, CA: Celestial Arts.
39. Judith, Anodea. 1996. Eastern Body, Western Mind: Psychology and the Chakra System as a Path to the Self. Berkeley, CA: Celestial Arts.
40. Saraswati, S. C. 2006. Drops of Nectar: Timeless Wisdom for Everyday Living. New Delhi: Wisdom Tree.
41. Hawkins, David. 1995. Power vs Force: The Hidden Determination of Human Behaviour. Sedona, Az: Veritas.
42. Katz, Dani. 2016. Yes, I Am. Charleston: Createspace.
43. Judith, Anodea. 1996. Eastern Body, Western Mind: Psychology and the Chakra System as a Path to the Self. Berkeley, CA: Celestial Arts.

About the Author

Dee Delaney is a mother writer yogi and lover of coffee. She lives in Goa India where she is researching and writing a trinity of books on unity consciousness called *The Truth is Within*. Book One: *The Truth – My Journey to the Other Side* deals with healing the Self through Eastern Philosophy and Jungian Psychotherapy. Book Two: *The Truth – Is the Art of Being*, looks into the eyes of death through the teachings of the Tibetan Bardo and The Pagan Book of Living and Dying. Book Three: *The Truth - Within the Heart of Love* explores unity consciousness and the alchemy of relationships. I discover the power of scared union, and the potential to ascend to the highest levels of being.

Dee lives and breathes this work, and the amazing stories and experiences she writes about have taken her across India to discover the fascinating truth about who she is and her life's purpose.

For now, she is focused on completing this work so she can share it with the world.

Whilst drinking lots of coffee of course!

About The Book

The Truth–My Journey to the Other Side is a book about love, loss, survival and healing. This is the story of how one woman survived the death of 3 partners, all young men in their 40s. How she picked herself off the floor and asked for help. How she faced heartache and healed her soul by walking through the darkness to come out the Other Side. In *The Truth–My Journey to the Other Side*, the author examines healing the Self through Eastern Philosophy and Jungian Psychotherapy.

As the story unfolds, she is forced to face her true 'Self' for the first time, and realises this suffering didn't happen To her, it happened For her, and her 'ordinary' life is transformed forever. *The Truth – My Journey to the Other Side* takes readers into the heart of their being and shows them a pathway to healing where love is stronger than death. This is one woman's story but also a universal story, because within us all is a spark of the divine that connects our heartbeats as one.

CPSIA information can be obtained
at www.ICGtesting.com
Printed in the USA
LVHW04s0729260518
578593LV00003B/4/P